The Boy
Grows Up

RICHARD McCANN

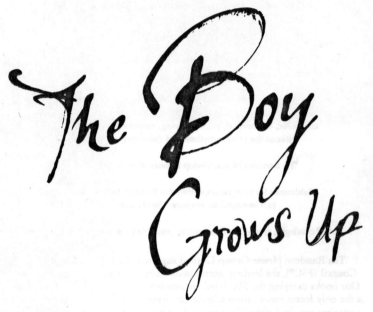

The Boy Grows Up

The Inspirational Story of his Journey
from Broken Boy to Family Man

EBURY
PRESS

5 7 9 10 8 6

Published in 2006 by Ebury Press, an imprint of Ebury Publishing
with the title *Into the Light*
This edition published 2007

Ebury Publishing is a division of the Random House Group

or otherwise,
ght owner

o. 954009

House Group
o.uk

the British Library

Forest Stewardship
fication organisation.
® certified paper. FSC
leading environmental
urement policy can be
onment

Typeset by seagulls.net
Printed and bound by CPI Group (UK) Ltd, Croydon, CR0 4YY

9780091908645

Change

Working daily, facing fears,

Releasing pain, allowing tears,

Letting go of inner hate,

Time for self. Special date,

Breaking habits, brand new choices,

Ignoring cruel, internal voices,

No mistakes, the past is past,

Just let go, break the cast!

Opened eyes, really seeing,

Dissolving blocks, spirit freeing,

Waking up to worldly needs,

Selfless acts, tender deeds,

Loving, spreading, joy and hope,

Looking up, expanded scope,

Reaching out to young and old,

Taking time, being bold,

Holding hands, giving, sharing,

Listening deeply, truly caring,

For Helen, with all my love

Contents

Prologue

'It's a shame your Dad's not around,' I said.

She just nodded, her mind more on the view than me.

'But this is the next best thing,' I went on, gesturing at the beautiful scenery surrounding the spot where her father's ashes were scattered.

She looked puzzled as I began to kneel down in front of her, still not understanding what I was doing. I nervously pulled the ring out of my pocket and took hold of her left hand.

'Will you marry me?'

I knelt there, waiting for my words to sink in, but she didn't reply. She just kept looking down at me, smiling ...

In the summer of 2002 I received a call telling me that my elder sister, Sonia, had stabbed her boyfriend, Jed, in self-defence after a weekend of violence. I was used to receiving phone calls from Sonia, or from other people, telling me what she had got up to, but this was the worst yet.

Trying to flee his brutal hands, she had met with a locked door and at that moment reached her breaking point. Picking up a knife, she thrust it into his chest, close to his heart. Many women in abusive relationships have found themselves at that point and will recognise the desperation and panic that forced Sonia to do what she did. In her case, charges were eventually dropped.

Such incidents are tidily labelled 'domestic violence' in police files, but the term is too sanitised. For some women, subjected to years of such trauma, the whole justice system appears to be stacked against them and there seems to be no way out. Once breaking point is reached, all reason is forgotten and, fearing for their lives, they lash out in primitive acts of self-defence.

It was when Sonia stabbed Jed that I decided to try and turn our lives around in a dramatic way and I wrote my first book, *Just a Boy*. I wanted to explain how Sonia had got to a point where she was able to commit such an extreme act, and I needed to do something that would make a difference to the way our family had become.

But things don't go as badly wrong as they have in our family overnight. The root of our troubles went back many years. It all began with the murder of our mother, Wilma

McCann, in 1975 at the hands of Peter Sutcliffe, the man who became known as the Yorkshire Ripper. At the time of Mum's death, Sonia, the oldest, was seven, I was five, and my younger sisters, Donna and Angela, were four and two.

I had heard that our parents' relationship was a complex and violent one, and that they had separated in 1974. My father, Gerry McCann, apparently walked out because of the constant arguing. Mum went on to another boyfriend, Keith, who beat her just as badly. In those early years in which a child develops, the years where our personalities are largely formed, we would witness drunken arguing and fights in which Mum often came off worse. Sporting bruises and black eyes, she would carry on with her life, doing her best to bring up her children and never leaving us in any doubt that she loved us dearly, although she received very little help and support, as most of her family lived in Scotland. She was not above picking a fight herself, however, but she was never violent towards us.

Sonia and I had woken in the early hours of a cold October morning in 1975 and walked to the local bus stop to wait for Mum to return home from a night on the town. We followed a path through a field behind our house, unaware that Mum's lifeless body lay just yards from our feet, shrouded by the early-morning darkness and mist.

By ending the life of our mother so cruelly and prematurely,

Peter Sutcliffe left our family a legacy which has followed us all to this day and will probably continue to do so until the end of our own lives.

Once Mum's body had been found, Sonia, Angela, Donna and I were taken into the care of the local authorities. After a few months of uncertainty, not to mention numerous failures by our father to turn up for promised weekend visits, we eventually set up home with Dad, his new girlfriend, Pauline, and their newborn baby, Cheryl. We were given no choice; the decision was made on our behalf by the authorities.

Only recently did I learn from one of Mum's sisters that her family had pleaded with the authorities to let us live with them in Scotland, placing two of us with one part of the family and two with another. Their requests were met with a brick wall of rejection. Dad was our next of kin, so it was considered his right to decide what was best for us, regardless of how he had behaved towards us and our mother in the past.

For the first few months we thought it was an adequate replacement life for the violent one we'd been living at home with Mum and her boyfriend. We thought our dad would look after us and protect us. We soon found out we were wrong. Before long, evidence of Dad's temper when in drink surfaced, and every one of us, including our new stepmum, experienced violence at his hands.

His mindless acts of bad temper and aggression included drowning Winnie, the pet dog, in the bath because it irritated him, and beating us all with sticks the thickness of chair legs. He often used to punish us by making us face the wall and place the palms of our hands on it. We would then have to crouch down, all the while keeping our palms flat on the wall. It was torture and our limbs screamed with pain within minutes, but we weren't allowed to move or he would threaten to kick us back into position. We always obeyed him.

Pauline did her best, considering she had to look after a newborn child and four severely traumatised children whose mother had been snatched away from them. At twenty-one she was little more than a child herself. What we needed was love and tenderness, understanding and compassion. Instead we ended up just existing from day to day, trying to keep on the right side of Dad.

He was a terrifying force as far as women and children were concerned, but his cruelty did not end with physical violence. He did not like us discussing Mum or what had happened to her. It was as if she had never existed. None of us were allowed to go to her funeral and we were never informed where she was buried. (I found out later in life when I overheard my father tell a friend.) Unable to comprehend or rationalise what had happened in our lives, we had to pretend that we had accepted she was gone and weren't going to remember her.

But I would never go through a day without thinking about her. The pain was almost unbearable. In *Just a Boy* I wanted to explain what it felt like to go through such a trauma as a small child, and to describe the long-term effects of a very public tragedy on our family, even the painful and embarrassing parts like Sonia's descent into alcoholism and my prison sentence for a drugs offence. I wanted it to be a 'warts and all' story, which showed how, despite everything, we had all survived.

But publication of the book was like detonating a bomb. Its success was colossal and it changed everything for me, but it forced us all to face our pasts. The consequences were dramatic and left me with a whole new set of problems as well as some incredible opportunities. The question was: would I be able to take advantage of those opportunities and heal some of the damage from the past?

In this book I have gone on another journey, into the parts of my past I didn't previously understand or know anything about. In writing it I wanted desperately to change the painful pictures in my head in order to move forward, and, by understanding what had happened to my mother and our family, finally to find peace and happiness.

chapter one

Finding a New Family

It was June 2003 and the heavens opened as we huddled under a few umbrellas at the graveside of Grandma Newlands, my mother's mother. It was a huge family gathering in Inverness with all seven of Mum's brothers, her three sisters and countless other relatives present. It had already been a long and emotional day. The hearse carrying my grandmother's coffin had taken a detour through the estate, 'The Ferry', where she had lived for so many years, and where she was well respected. Her children had followed in the black limousine and the rest of us drove behind in a convoy. I felt honoured to be part of such a large, close family and was struck by how much I looked like my mother's siblings. We all had the same deep-set eyes.

That day was a turning point for me. Although it was another attempt by me to say goodbye to Mum, at the same time I met a great many new relatives, some of whom I had known existed and others whom I knew nothing about. I don't know if Dad deliberately kept us separated from the Newlands family, or whether he just couldn't be bothered to keep in touch. Whatever his motivation, the results were the same and I was now meeting them as strangers.

After the burial we went back to the bungalow Grandma had only recently moved to. Everyone started talking and taking photographs, not knowing when they would all be together again in one place. The thick Scottish accents of my aunts mingled with the more varied voices of their brothers who had travelled down into England many years before.

'Your mum's family were all tinkers and gypsies,' Dad would tell us dismissively if ever we asked, as if that was a good enough reason to have nothing to do with them. Now, as I listened to the family history directly from them, I learned that Mum's ancestors had indeed been itinerant labourers, travelling from one area to another, seeking whatever work was available. Often they would labour on farms when there was a demand for extra hands at harvesting times, sometimes they would join road-building gangs. But to my ears their way of life sounded noble and romantic, certainly not to be scoffed at. My grandparents were grafters, unlike Dad, who would drift in and out of work when he felt like it and didn't have a hangover. To me, being itinerant seemed a great deal more admirable than being idle.

Travelling back to Scotland, both geographically and through time, jogged a long-forgotten memory of visiting a farm with Mum. I can't have been more than four at the time and I had had no idea where the farm might have been.

'Is it likely that I have memories of coming to Scotland as a child?' I asked.

'Your mum often jumped on a train and headed up to Inverness,' my aunts told me, 'to be with her parents for a few days of respite. What do you remember?'

'I can picture an old stone farmhouse with a very large building at the back where they stored hay. I remember being sat in the deep furrows made by a complicated, dangerous-looking piece of machinery hooked on the back of a tractor. I was running my hands through the soil.' Finding potatoes in the soil had felt like unearthing hidden treasure; a game for a small boy, but hard toil for the adults who depended on a good crop for a living wage. They all nodded as they listened to me, and told me that the farm I was thinking of was about eight miles from Inverness. So it was a real memory.

Uncles, aunts and cousins happily regaled me with stories

about Mum and the things she'd got up to as a girl and a young mother. Their eagerness to reminisce about her was a stark contrast to my father's insistence on pretending she never existed. For years I'd wanted so desperately to talk about the most important person in my life, to keep the memory of her alive, but had been forced to remain silent. This Newlands family gathering was like a feast after a long, agonising famine. Now I started to see Mum's death through the eyes of her parents and siblings rather than exclusively through my own eyes, and those of her other children.

At first I found it a little presumptuous to call them 'my family' after being kept away from most of them for so long. Even though it hadn't been my choice or my fault, I felt I'd been denying their existence for most of my life. I knew that if I could have turned the clock back to the days after Mum died and if anyone had asked me who I wanted to live with, with hindsight I would have chosen to spend my childhood with these open, welcoming people rather than with our father. But no one told me about them, let alone that they had tried to claim custody of us. And what would I have known anyway? I was five years old and unable to understand what was going on around me.

But Mum's family understood only too well what kind of person Dad could be.

———

'We'd seen your mum beaten black and blue at his hands,' my aunts told me. 'We feared the same would happen to you.'

As it dawned on me that they had never rejected and abandoned me as I had assumed, I warmed more and more to them, asking endless questions about the past, eager to make up for lost time.

'Your grandparents came from the islands off the north-east coast of Scotland. They were married on a small island called Bow in the Orkney Isles,' one aunt told me. 'Some of your uncles were born closer to Norway than Scotland.'

These snapshots of a family history seemed to come from a different world to the one I was used to in inner city Leeds. It was a world of family pride and togetherness, good humour and a sense of tradition.

Sonia had not attended the funeral and I knew one day that she would regret it. On the journey back to Leeds my mind drifted back to our childhood in Bramley with Dad. It must have been obvious to our teachers that our family and the Dudleys who lived two doors away didn't have much in the way of a disposable income. One year we were given letters to take home to our parents inviting us to go to The Leeds Children's Holiday Camp. The camp was at Silverdale, close to Morecambe Bay on the west coast. It had been set up before the war for children whose families fell below the poverty line. In years gone by it had been embarrassingly named, "Leeds Poor Children's Holiday Camp" and children were weighed before they went. After two weeks of good food they were weighed again when they returned. Most, not surprisingly, had put on considerable amounts of weight.

I was happy to be chosen, and even more delighted with the news that the Dudley boys were going too. For most of us, it was our first holiday. We were more excited than we had ever felt before.

The first thing we were asked to do on arrival was to strip naked and form a queue in the corridor. Whilst trying our best to cover ourselves, we were each given the uniform we were going to have to wear for the two weeks of our stay; grey shorts, socks and black sweaters.

The days were filled with hours of playing out in the camp's grounds, which consisted of an outdoor pool, swings and a wooded area where boys could run as wild as they liked. The nights consisted of watching films in the small cinema or attending discos in the hall. We would also visit local places of interest like The Wishing Well, The Pepper-Pot or a trip down the coast to enter the "eerie caves", which were reputed to be haunted.

Many of the other boys were shy and found it difficult making new friends, so I was relieved to have the Dudley boys there and to be part of a big, happy, boisterous group.

Having experienced losing someone, I always find myself watching to see how other people cope with similar tragedies. Most, I've realised, do cope in their own ways, but those who don't need all the help they can get. Nothing can prepare any of us for the devastation we feel when the news of a death first sinks in but eventually, maybe two, ten or in my case almost thirty years later, we learn how to adapt, accept and move forward, driven by the human spirit and its will to survive.

The pain is made all the more unbearable by the death of someone young and seemingly healthy because it's so unexpected. As I sank further and further into my own thoughts I wondered if the risk of grief was the price we all had to pay for entering into relationships and making attachments, which inevitably involved loss, either through death, separation or parents letting go of their children.

The first thing we do when we hear of a death is search for rational explanations to make the news more understandable and I remember as a five year old doing just that. I felt back then that Mum had been a sacrifice to give us a better life. How wrong I was.

After the loss of my own mother when I was a child, the pain would return when I felt a subsequent loss, like when a girl-friend would end a relationship, particularly in my late teens and early twenties. It seemed to be compounded by the devas-tation I felt when I lost Mum and resonated afresh each time.

I had lost so much through my life, starting with Mum and the security and love which she had given me. I then lost the ability to be myself; Dad saw to that. I lost the confidence that I had as a young boy, and when I went to prison for dealing in drugs I lost my freedom. I almost lost the home that I cherished when I came out of prison and, for a brief moment, I lost the will to live, as I planned the suicide pact with my elder sister, Sonia. Somehow I had managed to deal with all these losses along the way and had come out the other side.

I remembered the feeling from years before, when I'd tried to cope with my mother's death. Was this my mind's way of dealing with death, keeping the pain at arm's length?

I could often imagine the range of emotions that people who lost loved ones, especially those whose lives were cut short, might experience. They might assume there would be a solution to their pain; that something would happen to take it away and that life would then return to how it had been before. Then a new pain would rise up when they realised that no such solution would ever be possible; that there would be no cure for what they were suffering. I had witnessed many young deaths over the years, one of my younger sisters boyfriends died aged seventeen in a freak accident, another thirty two year old friend of Sonia and I had been found drowned in a local river a couple of years ago, probably one of Sonia's closest friends and I had known a couple of old friends who had committed suicide over the years. Part of the pain comes from knowing that nothing you can do will ever make a difference to the deceased now.

I wondered how my own father would have felt if I had been successful with my plans to kill myself when I left prison. I wondered if he would have felt guilty about my death.

I was beginning to see a pattern as to how the human spirit deals with unplanned tragedies and losses, and how we work through the pain until we are finally able to accept what has happened and move on.

We are almost prepared for the loss of the elderly, once they've lived long and fruitful lives. But when someone young dies it blindsides us and throws us into total shock. They would have to adapt to a new understanding of the world, which would contain memories of a loved one and an irrational longing to wake up and discover this had been some awful nightmare.

That was how I had felt when Mum died. A week later it was my sixth birthday and the staff in Becketts Park Children's home did their best to give me a present and have some form of celebration. But the only thing I wanted was to have my loving mother back beside me. For thirty years I've been wanting to wake up from that nightmare.

chapter two

The Good Samaritan

All the time I was writing *Just a Boy* I was aware that it might prove to be a waste of time, that it was possible no one else would be interested in my story. Once I'd received a firm offer from a publisher for the book, however, I realised I was being given an opportunity to completely transform my life, although I couldn't work out what direction I wanted to take it in. I knew that over the years I had been trying to find help to overcome some of the pain of my childhood and now I felt I could eliviate the pain others felt but didn't know how I could go about it.

I wanted to do something positive towards alleviating this pain, but didn't know how I should go about it. I had no training in counselling. I hadn't even had much of an education, having left school at the first possible opportunity. I decided I would start by contacting Samaritans and asking if they would consider me as a volunteer. I remembered calling them myself once when I was at a low ebb and they had been a lifeline to me that night. I'd been watching the television when a scene came on in which a prostitute was murdered in a way that reminded me of Mum. It had affected me deeply and I'd needed someone to talk to. I knew how much that person had helped me and I wanted to have a chance to do the same for others.

I rang to find out about the joining procedure and was invited to a group interview. I went along, feeling very nervous. We were all asked to sit round a table. Some small cards had been placed face down on the surface in front of us. Once we'd introduced ourselves we each had to turn over a card and say a little about the subject written on it. I found all the subjects easy to comment on until prostitution came up. My stomach muscles instantly tightened and my mouth became dry. For so many years I'd had to read in the papers how the Ripper's victims had been prostitutes, including Mum. Other children at school used to ask me if it was true. I never denied it, believing that if the press said so, then it must be right. In time I learned that it wasn't that clear cut and that the press had merely lumped many of the victims under one label.

The first time it was said on television, one of Mum's brothers, Isaac, and his then wife, Vicky, contacted Yorkshire Television, outraged, and insisted they apologise on air and admit the allegation was untrue. They did apologise, but the label still stuck, particularly when later victims turned out to be on the game. It was hopeless trying to fight the slur against her character once the national press started repeating it. It didn't matter to me what Mum had done in that way, she was still my mum, but I knew that society looked down on prostitutes and I didn't want anyone looking down on her. In writing *Just a Boy* I felt as though I'd finally vindicated Mum by explaining her lifestyle and what a loving mother she was.

After our group interview we each went individually to another room with two Samaritan volunteers. I was still feeling a little uncomfortable. But the interview was low-key and relaxed and I thought I was doing well until one of them asked me how the group session had gone. I had to be honest and say that one of the subjects had unsettled me.

'Which one?' they asked.

'Prostitution.'

Now I felt even worse, imagining they would think I was a user of prostitutes. I tried to explain, feeling as if I was being interrogated under a spotlight. It was hopeless. My mouth became too dry to talk and I just wanted the interview to end so

I could drive back to the safety of my home. They thanked me for sharing such a personal thing with them and told me I would hear from them within the next week or so. I explained I was going on holiday the following Friday in the hope they would let me know their decision before I went.

I felt terrible. Although I really wanted to have succeeded, it was one of the worst interviews I'd ever given. But I truly believed I would be good at the job. I felt I'd always been sympathetic to other people's problems and found it easy to empathise with them, maybe because of the pain I'd felt as a young boy and from so often feeling like the underdog. There had been many occasions when I'd been proud of myself for standing up for someone being bullied, or made a stand against someone for being racist. At one of the companies I'd worked for there'd been quite a culture of racism. It was 'black bastards' this or 'pakkis' that. It infuriated me but I remained silent because I was new to the company and most of the time it was the team leader who was the guilty one. It was particularly difficult to listen to as my half-sister Cheryl had a mixed race daughter. She was a lovely child and each time I heard a comment I thought of her. Once I'd been with the company a few months I rustled up enough courage to speak out.

'Can I just say something to you all?' I said, although I was actually aiming it at the team leader. 'I have a mixed race niece and when you speak in this way it offends me.'

'You what?' shrieked the team leader, immediately adding another racist remark.

I was boiling inside but knew I was the odd one out. Taking a deep breath, with my heart thumping, I repeated what I'd said and asked if they would refrain from speaking like this, at least when I was around. The team leader jumped out of his seat and started shouting at me.

'Who the fuck do you think you are coming in here with your views? We've never had any blacks or pakkis working here and it'll always be that way.'

'I'd like to see you say that in front of my niece's father,' was all I could think of saying, which infuriated him even more.

'Are you threatening me?' he demanded.

My stomach was churning. Things were about to turn nasty. I stood. 'I don't have to listen to this,' I said, and walked out of the door.

This scene had been played out in full view of everyone in the canteen, including the union rep, who'd been sitting in front of us. I tried to get on with my work that afternoon but I was too furious to be able to concentrate. A little later the union rep asked if I wanted to take it any further. I told him I didn't. I'd made my point and knew I would never get an apology. I also knew that nothing I could say or do would change the man's opinions.

By the time I went on the holiday I still hadn't heard from Samaritans, which was disappointing. I was sure I had a lot to give them and just wanted a chance to show them that I was capable.

But when I returned from Spain I found a letter waiting for me. Holding my breath as I tore it open, I had to read it a couple of times before taking in what they were telling me. My interview had been successful and I was to start the training a few weeks later.

It was brilliant news. Someone believed I could be a good and useful influence on others. All the experiences I had been through could be harnessed to help people. I couldn't wait to get my teeth into the work.

In recent years I'd worked as a buyer in the rag trade, which had served its purpose in giving me a living and enabling me to keep my house from being repossessed when I came out of prison, but I'd become disillusioned by it. I knew I would feel more job satisfaction helping others than lining the pockets of shareholders and, at the back of my mind, I had a small thought that if ever I got the opportunity, I would pursue some sort of full-time caring career, using my experiences in life to help others. I wasn't yet sure how I would be able to make the change, but I knew that joining Samaritans would be a big step in the right direction, increasing my work experience and showing my commitment to this line of work.

I started my training with six other newcomers, all women, not knowing what to expect but excited by the challenge. The trainers started by explaining how to handle calls, the correct procedure to follow, concentrating on the caller's feelings, and on how to deal with such things as a suicide caller, a bomb warning or a face-to-face visitor. We then took it in turns to role-play a scenario in which the trainer would play the part of a distressed caller and each of us would sit in a booth and try to deal with the call. The resulting conversation was relayed to all the other trainees in another room. We would then discuss each of our calls and give one another feedback on our performances.

The practice calls started gently with a call from a young person who'd fallen out with a friend. They then progressed through to calls from someone who'd been unfaithful with her brother-in-law and a lady who'd been given the news she had a month to live and couldn't tell her family. There was a call from a woman who'd discovered her son was gay and another from a caller who'd been abused as a child and had taken some tablets. It dawned on me that we would soon be talking to people who would be suffering from a multitude of extremely distressing situations – this was no longer a game, it was a rehearsal for real life.

Once my training was complete I chose a shift and met my new team. At first I listened to a few calls to get a feel for it, but I knew I just needed to get on the phone and speak to someone in order to put my training to good use. I started taking calls that afternoon and was surprised how much easier it was compared to the training, when six others had been listening in. Now it was just the callers and me. I took a long call from a very distressed lady who had definitely had a worse childhood than mine. It was a good feeling to know that there were other people who were finding ways to cope with difficulties which I knew, from first-hand experience, could sometimes seem insurmountable. I quickly learned there were a lot of people out there who had suffered and were still suffering, many more than I had ever imagined. The more I discovered the surer I was that I had made the right decision.

I was surprised by what a hard grind it was physically. Although my regular shift was from 6 p.m. to 10 p.m., we sometimes did overnight duties on a weekend, which started at 10 p.m. and finished at 8 a.m. I wasn't prepared for how gruelling this would be. I reminded myself that I'd grown used to working such hours in the army, so there was no reason why

I shouldn't be able to do it again. My body would be trying to shut down and sleep around midnight, but the calls would continue to come. A call at 1 a.m. would finish and I would struggle to stay awake as soon as I'd hung up, but would find myself alert again as soon as the phone rang a few minutes later, and then at regular intervals throughout the night. This was far worse than the guard duty I'd done when I was in the army. At least there you were given a four-hour rest in between each period of duty.

Once morning arrived I would drive home and collapse straight into bed, exhausted and usually satisfied but sometimes troubled by the things I'd heard during the night.

chapter three

Another Suicide Attempt

However satisfying it felt to be helping others through my work at Samaritans, there was one person I still wanted to help more than any other. But it seemed the more pressure I put on Sonia to stop drinking the more she drank. I was fighting a losing battle.

Discovering her heavily drunk at home once again about six months after I had started at Samaritans, I stormed out of the house, feeling I couldn't go on seeing her like that. I had loved Sonia unconditionally for years. She could get drunk, hurl abuse at me, disappear, cause me worry, but I would always go back to her. She needed someone in her life that she could turn to for help and I owed it to her to be that person because of the way she had protected me as a small child.

On this occasion I left her for a couple of days and on the third day I got home from work to find a message on my answering machine. Long silences suggested she was still drunk, then she muttered, 'Sorry.'

My heart sank. I guessed she'd been drinking solidly since I walked out. I knew instantly by her tone she was at rock bottom and would be thinking the only way out of her pain would be to end her life. I had to get to her before she did something stupid. It had been a few hours since she left the message and I prayed I wasn't already too late.

As I drove to her house I had to force myself to keep within the speed limit. The journey took twenty minutes. I knocked nervously and tried the door handle. It was open. I walked in, calling her name, and pushed open the living-room door. My heart was in my mouth. I was terrified of what I might find. The house was completely silent, making the alarm bells in my head ring even louder. Empty lager cans were strewn over the living-room floor, and the light fitting had been torn from the ceiling. Sonia was nowhere to be seen. I spotted an A4 lined piece of paper on the coffee table and snatched it up. It read: '*Dear Richard, I have to go now. I want you to know I love all my family. Lots of love, Sonia.*'

I read the note again to make sure I wasn't being overdramatic, and knew I'd been right to drive over immediately.

Dropping it back on the table, I ran upstairs, terrified I'd got there too late and was going to find Sonia dead. Panicked, I threw open each of the bedroom doors, rushing from one room to the next, half expecting to see her hanging somewhere. While I was serving my time in prison, I found a man hanging in his cell. Although he survived, I would never forget the sight. I don't think such images are ever erased from one's memory. How would I cope if I found Sonia like that and I was too late to save her?

She wasn't upstairs. Running out of the house, I got into my car, reversed out onto the road and headed towards Angela's, thinking she might be there. Then, as I approached the main road, something caught my eye. A thin woman was stumbling down the road towards me.

The moment I realised it was Sonia the tension left me. If she was alive I still had another chance to turn her round and push her away from the pit of despair. I took some deep breaths, knowing I had to watch every word I said and treat her gently if I was going to get her cooperation. As Sonia made her way back to the house I slowly parked up the car, got out and locked it as though I was just arriving for the first time.

'Hi, how are you?' I asked.

'Upset,' she replied.

'Come on, let's have a cup of tea.'

I followed her in, ignoring the fallen light fitting and note on the table, acting as though I'd just popped in to see her, forcing myself to remain calm. I spent a couple of hours with her and then went to use the toilet upstairs. It was then, as I passed the open door, that I noticed a thin rope hanging from the ceiling in the smallest bedroom. I hadn't spotted it earlier in my rush to find a body. The rope hung from a hatch above the bed, and on the bed was a small bedside cabinet. It looked as though Sonia had prepared the cabinet to stand on, so she could kick it out from underneath her once the noose was round her neck. How could I have missed something so noticeable?

'Sonia!' I shouted, all my self-control deserting me. 'What have you been doing?'

She came upstairs to the bedroom and just stood in front of me.

'What have you been doing, Sonia?' I repeated.

'Don't start,' she warned.

I sat down on the bed, resting my back against the wall, and started crying, picturing how it must have been as she lurched around in her drunken state, all alone in the house, trying to arrange her own death. What chance did I have of saving her? I couldn't be there for her every minute of the day and if she put her mind to it then she would do this again.

Next time she might not bother to ring and alert me. Sonia sat down beside me.

'I'm sorry,' she said.

We hugged one another, both crying, both telling the other how much we loved them, neither of us knowing what to do or what to say.

'How could I live without you?' I asked.

'I'm sorry. I won't do anything silly.'

We sat there on the bed together, hugging each other for at least five minutes.

'Shall we go downstairs and make another cup of tea?' I suggested eventually.

Sonia brightened up and nodded.

'You go and put the kettle on,' I said.

Once she'd gone I climbed on the bed and raised my hands to the hatchway in the ceiling, which was used to access the loft. I pushed the small square door up and to the side. I could see the rope was tied to a beam in the loft area. Without saying anything I went back downstairs, fetched a large knife from the kitchen drawer and returned to cut the rope so there was no way she could try again, not with that rope at least. She didn't question my actions, just got on with making the tea.

I stayed with her until she'd convinced me she was OK and no longer looking into the abyss, then I drove home, knowing in my heart that one day she just might succeed in taking her own life, or would come to some other harm while in a drunken state. I dreaded the thought of having to learn to live without her in the same way I'd had to learn to live without Mum.

After that, I tried to get my head down at work and continue with my day-to-day routine, but at the back of my mind there was always the worry that Sonia was going to do something stupid. The previous year I'd convinced her she needed to get herself into detoxification, but the place she booked into asked her to leave after ten weeks, when they caught her smoking one of the other residents' joints. She'd been drinking ever since and I knew I couldn't help her myself.

I rang the detox unit again and asked the nurse if they would allow me to bring Sonia in to give it another go. She said they couldn't do that since she'd been asked to leave the previous year.

'So, what am I supposed to do, as her brother, when she's drinking and threatening to take her own life?' I asked, unable to hide how upset I was.

After some time the nurse agreed that if Sonia were to show willing by visiting the local Alcoholics Anonymous, then they would consider admitting her again. It was a chink of light in the gloom. I couldn't wait to let Sonia know we had a possible way out, but when I told her they weren't going to readmit her without conditions, she took it personally.

'They can go to hell!' she spat.

I was going to have to think of something else.

chapter four

Talking to Dad

As the publication date of *Just a Boy* drew closer I became more nervous. Was I doing the right thing by exposing myself and the family to the whole world? I wavered between excitement at the prospect of such a major achievement, and abject terror at the thought of having to talk in public and in the media about such intensely personal issues.

I knew that some time soon I was going to have to sit down with my father and explain why I'd decided to write my life story. I felt I had to pre-warn him of the things I was going to expose, particularly the parts that would tell the truth about him and his behaviour towards us. But I kept putting it off. The revelations about him were going to shock a lot of people, his own family included, who thought Gerry McCann was a 'great guy' and a 'comedian'. It was only those of us who had to live with him who knew his true colours. When he was drunk, which was often, he became a foul-mouthed, belligerent bully towards all the women and children in the family. Having grown up and escaped his tyranny, I was very reluctant to go back and risk a confrontation, but it had to be done.

Writing *Just a Boy* was like shedding a skin and I felt the most liberated I'd ever felt. Until then I'd been living my life as an adult in much the same way as I'd done as a child, giving everyone around me the impression that I was fine. I'd wanted them to believe that what they saw was what they got. But it wasn't the case. I was still living two lives, one the cheerful outer persona and the other the true self with all the history and the painful memories. Now the book was written I didn't have to hide anything because people would finally understand what I'd been through. Baring my soul was a big risk but I knew I had to do it.

I'd also had to admit that I'd been to prison, and I was worried about how people who I'd met since those times would react to that revelation. But, I told myself, almost ten years had passed since the offence and I'd done all I could to distance myself from living such a negative existence, concentrating on the more positive aspects to life. If people chose to judge me for my crimes there was nothing I could do about it. I was just going to have to wait and see what happened next.

———

One of my greatest escapes, and methods of relaxation, is salsa dancing. I still go regularly and can't imagine life without that outlet. It has helped me a great deal over the years, and I've also made some great friends through it, people who are very different from my family.

One of the things that has always appealed to me is that for the four or five minutes I am dancing with a woman, I feel completely free. The only thing I have to think about is enjoying the music and leading my partner correctly so that she also enjoys the dance. There are never enough men to go round, so the dancing is continuous for those of us who are there, and concentrating on the steps leaves no room for worries about work, about Sonia or about Dad, and for memories about Mum or Sutcliffe. I guess Sonia would use drink, and in the past I had used drugs, to achieve the same effect.

One evening at my salsa club, when I was sitting down trying to catch my breath between dances, I noticed in the bar a man who used to date one of Dad's sisters. He was a nice enough guy and after he spotted me he came over and sat at my table. It was obvious he was drinking but not enough that he was causing any embarrassment.

'What are you doing in a place like this?' he asked, gesturing to the couples still on the dance floor.

It was not the sort of place anyone else in our family would ever come to by choice, which was another reason I liked it. I preferred to keep these two aspects of my life separate.

'Salsa's one of my hobbies,' I explained. 'I've been doing it for years.'

He was dumbfounded and seemed to be having trouble believing that Gerry McCann's son would ever be found in such a place, doing such a thing. At the same time he seemed impressed.

'It's great to see you in company with so many nice people,' he said once the truth had sunk in.

There were three or four women at my table and he asked which one was with me.

'They're all friends,' I explained.

He seemed not to be able to understand the concept of being with women who were just friends.

'Gerry would be proud of you,' he said eventually.

My stomach turned at the mention of my father's name. I'd only just finished writing about the things he'd done to us all, raking over the memories and opening the wounds. I was at salsa to forget about all that.

'Don't talk to me about him,' I said, going on to explain how ashamed of Dad I was and that if he had come into this bar while I was there I would have died. Having started, I went on to tell him how Dad was not the person everyone thought he was, that he'd treated us all badly and shirked his responsibilities as a father.

I guessed there was a chance my comments would find their way back to Dad, but I didn't care. I had no respect for him and didn't care who knew it. But the confrontation made me realise that I couldn't put off the meeting with him any longer. I didn't want him to read about the book or be told what was in it by one of his relatives. He should hear about it from me. I owed him that at least. I knew he still saw me as a boy, even though I was now thirty-four, approaching the age he'd been when I'd finally left home. I was a man now and I had to sit down man-to-man and tell him what I thought of him.

I phoned him and we spoke for almost two hours, me shouting and being angry at one moment, and pitying him the next.

'What I'd like,' I said eventually, 'is if we could all meet somewhere for a meal, without alcohol, behaving like a family who cared for one another.'

'Well, I want to be able to do things like that, too,' he replied.

'I'll try to arrange for us all to meet so we can attempt to bridge the gaps,' I said, although I wasn't sure Dad would even know how to do normal family things. I doubted it would ever happen.

* * *

Over the next few weeks I suggested to Sonia, Donna and Angela that it might be a good idea if we could all meet up with Dad and become a family. None of them was interested, so the idea was forgotten. I knew, however, that I still had to talk to him about the book so I suggested he and I go to the greyhound racing in Sheffield.

We'd kept greyhounds when I was a child, and Dad took me hunting rabbits on a couple of occasions in the local woods. Wanting to defuse the situation a little, I arranged for Olga, an ex-girlfriend of mine, to join us, to give me a bit of moral support.

Olga and I picked Dad up from his flat. I'd never actually arranged to meet Dad over the years, not even for a drink. I could count on both hands the number of times we'd met up and it was normally because we'd bumped into one another in pubs.

The three of us drove down the motorway to Sheffield. There always seemed to be reminders of Sutcliffe and what he had done wherever I turned, even now. This drive reminded me that Sheffield was where he'd been caught back in 1981.

We had a reasonable night and Olga thought Dad didn't seem to be the same person she'd read about when I first showed her the early chapters of *Just a Boy*.

'That's exactly what most people think about him,' I told her. 'It's not until you've lived with him and experienced his drunken rages that you see his alter ego.'

When the night was over we headed back up the motorway to Leeds and dropped Olga off before I drove Dad home to his flat. But I didn't speak about my feelings or thoughts on how he'd brought us up. I still didn't feel ready for it. That would have to wait until we next met.

This was over a drink on a Saturday afternoon. Finally it felt like the right moment to say exactly what I wanted to say.

'Why did you drown Winnie in the bath?' I asked, having plucked up all my courage.

I remembered the incident so clearly it could have been yesterday. Our pet dog had been scraping on the front door after being chased by a group of local dogs because she was in season. He'd snatched her up, carried her upstairs, ran the bath and drowned her with his bare hands. Although I was devastated at the time, I'd always been too frightened to utter a word about it until now.

'I come from a different world to you,' he said, dismissing the incident. 'In Northern Ireland I was involved in breeding greyhounds and it was commonplace to drown a new litter of pups if they were surplus to requirements.'

'That's rubbish,' I retorted. 'This was the family pet, who we all loved. What had Winnie done to deserve being drowned?'

'She was on heat and causing all sorts of trouble.'

'But you should have been a responsible adult and taken her to the vet to have her doctored.'

'We couldn't afford things like vets' fees,' he grumbled.

'If you could afford to drink every day you could afford a visit to the vet,' I pointed out.

He'd been drinking on the afternoon when he decided to kill the dog. He'd nearly always been drinking when he acted violently.

'What about the time you tried to drown me in the bath, then?' I went on, determined to pin him down to admitting responsibility for something. 'And how about when you took a stick to Angela?'

'I just wanted to frighten you, so you'd not do anything wrong again.'

'Well, that worked.' I almost laughed. 'We were all petrified of you. We were terrified of making the wrong move, of saying the wrong thing or of looking at you in the wrong way. You may not have been violent to us all the time, but we lived in fear of you all the time, which felt just as bad. Don't you understand? We'd lost our mother in the worst way possible and we needed the love of a parent who was going to see we got the support we needed. We had enough to be frightened of, we didn't need anything else.'

A few tables away from us was a family with a child who looked to be about six or seven.

'It was a week before my sixth birthday when Mum was

murdered,' I went on, trying to make him see. 'Imagine if that little girl, who's happily playing with her parents, was to have her mother murdered by a serial killer tonight. Isn't it obvious she'd need years of love and care from whoever was looking after her? That she would be affected for the rest of her life?'

'Yes, well, I know that now,' he muttered, as if trying to end the conversation, 'but things were different then.'

'That's bollocks! Any reasonable adult would know that something like that would affect a child for ever. And you chose to punish us the way you did, with sticks and physical tortures. Dad, that was child abuse.'

'Well, maybe it would be seen that way now, but back then it wasn't.'

He had an answer for everything. He was living in denial. It was as if he just couldn't accept his wrongdoing and truly believed he had behaved acceptably. He eventually admitted that some of the things he did were wrong but wouldn't admit to any of them specifically.

'All families have their secrets,' he said, 'and they should remain in the family.' Then, trying a different tack, 'I never knew what you were going through. Why didn't you tell me?'

'How could I have told you anything? You weren't the kind of person I felt I could turn to in those early years.'

I finally got on to the subject of the book. I explained I

needed to write it for me to lay my past to rest, as well as to clear Mum's name.

'The press have portrayed her as some kind of reckless mother who didn't care for her children,' I said. 'Yes, I know she was a little reckless in the last few months, but she paid for that mistake with her life. This is my chance to tell the world what a loving mother she was. That's a lot more important than sparing your feelings.'

I knew the things I'd said in the book would hurt him but I reasoned he was responsible for his violence and that my needs were more important than his. I was still angry with him for causing so much damage to the children who lived with him. After we'd all left home he'd had another three children with Pauline, and I thought she'd done the brave and right thing by leaving him, so that her younger children never had to live with the constant fear we'd all been subjected to.

'I'm not happy for you to be writing about our lives,' he said, eventually. 'But if it's what you need to do, then go for it. I'm proud of you.'

We finished our drinks and I said goodbye. Dad threw his arms round me.

'I love you, son,' he said.

Maybe the book was actually going to bring us closer together after all these years.

---

chapter five

Meeting Others

The satisfaction I was experiencing working with Samaritans was making me think of other ways in which I might be able to help people, particularly those who were going through experiences similar to mine. I decided to contact SAMM – Support After Murder and Manslaughter. I'd first rung the organisation ten years earlier, having heard about them after seeing a particularly distressing murder in a television drama, and I now felt I would like to become more involved. Until that point the only contact I'd had with them was receiving a quarterly newsletter.

I rang the number on the newsletter and a softly spoken lady calling herself Pamela answered the phone. I asked if she could give me details of my local SAMM group, so I could meet others who'd been through similar experiences to me.

'I feel as though I'm moving forward now,' I explained, 'and I'd welcome the chance to meet others.'

'I'm afraid there isn't a group in your area,' Pamela informed me, going on to ask me about myself and about which member of my family had been murdered.

After we'd been speaking for some time she asked if I'd be interested in forming a group in Leeds myself.

'But I don't have any experience of that sort of thing,' I protested.

'You've had all the experience you need,' she reassured me, 'having lived with the fact of your mum being murdered. Why don't you come down to a training session in London next month?'

Since I was hoping to meet other people with similar experiences and wanted to do something positive with what I'd been through, I agreed. I felt it was time to take the things that had been so negative in my life and use them to help others who had recently been bereaved. Maybe I could start a group, or at least explore the possibilities. My confidence was growing all the time and I now felt able to tackle challenges I would never have dreamed of attempting a year or two before.

One month later, I made my way to the designated London hotel for the evening meeting that was to take place before the training session the next day. I was feeling very nervous about who I was likely to meet and how they would react to me. I eventually found the group in the restaurant. They'd just finished eating and were joking noisily, just like any other bunch of friends, which surprised me. Quite unreasonably, I'd expected them to be sitting around looking sombre and feeling sorry for themselves. Finding them in high spirits was both a surprise and a relief. I immediately felt comfortable being with people who had been through the same experiences I had. I knew I was never going to have to try to explain how I felt about things – they already understood.

I was shocked to come across a girl I once knew from my salsa club in Leeds. She was called Michaela. I had seen her often at salsa, and had once gone with her and a group of other friends to a late-night café after the dancing had ended. We'd lost touch over the years, and now here she was with her sister and mother. She told me that her father had been murdered by a friend of the family.

No one except Pamela knew who in my family had been murdered and they were all happy for me to tell them my story if and when I was ready. Before long we moved from the restaurant and sat together in the hotel lounge. Most of them seemed to know one another already and started to talk about their own situations. Listening in, I found their losses varied. Some had lost husbands, others had lost sons or daughters, and they all had their own tragic stories to tell. We sat into the early hours of the morning, talking about how we felt without the usual fear of anyone being judgemental.

The next day we all met again for breakfast, still in a relatively jovial mood. Afterwards we gathered in the conference room and the official meeting started. It was sad we had to meet under such terrible circumstances but I was glad I'd made the effort to come. We were all there because we were interested in setting up local support groups. I could see I was going to get as much out of a group as anyone else there.

As different people spoke of their experiences there were light moments as well, like the woman who told us how she'd once put her shoes in the fridge, her mind distracted after hearing her terrible news. Such incidents seemed to be normal when people were coping with sudden tragedy.

At the end of the day we all went away to think more about how we would go about setting up our own groups. My initial problem was that each group required three members to run it. At that stage I was the only person from the Leeds area interested in becoming involved. I would have to think how I was going to include others. I suggested to Pamela she put a small advertisement in the next newsletter and she agreed. I understood that setting up the group would take some time, since the newsletter was only quarterly, but I felt certain that one day we would have our own successful SAMM group in Leeds.

I also had to start thinking about a location for the group. I was determined to overcome these obstacles and make it work. It would be worth any amount of effort if it helped just one person. I'd started noticing how many stories there were in the papers about murders. It had become such a common occurrence it no longer caused the same level of shock it had in the past. It was definitely on the increase, especially with the rise in gun crime.

I read in one newspaper that sixteen people were murdered each week in Britain and the headline stated that we were now living in 'Murder Country'. The police, it seemed, were just as powerless to stop this rise in gun crime as they had been to catch Mum's killer almost thirty years earlier.

In the past I'd often thought about contacting children of the Ripper's other victims, but lacked the confidence, believing it wouldn't be possible to find them and that they might not want to hear from me anyway. However, the idea continued to play on my mind. Sonia had also told me she'd often wondered about them. I knew they must be around somewhere and that we were all contactable by the police due to a payment we all received back in 1990 from *Private Eye* magazine, after there was an appeal to its readers to raise funds to make a £600,000 libel payment to Sonia Sutcliffe. When the payment was reduced to £60,000 on appeal, the excess money was divided up and paid to the victims' families. It was the police who contacted us at the time and I thought about writing to the families using this route. Eventually I decided I would try to find out more about them first.

Once *Just a Boy* was published – and I already knew there was going to be quite a bit of publicity surrounding the event – I imagined most of the other victims' children would have at least heard about me, or maybe even got hold of a copy to read. This gave me more confidence to go ahead with my search. I felt it should now also be possible to use the Internet to find them. I decided to do it and set about trying to identify all the children by name, scouring every book about the Yorkshire Ripper that had ever been published.

I tracked down all the relevant titles and was even able to find a copy of a title that had been taken off the shelves due to another libel issue with Sonia Sutcliffe. The publisher later admitted the allegations to be wholly untrue and had promised to destroy all future copies of the book. It was also reported that Sonia Sutcliffe had brought no less than nine libel claims over the years.

The most recent book to be published was *Wicked Beyond Belief* by Michael Bilton, and it was this I used most as I set about trying to discover the identities of the other children. It was the first time I'd ever read about the family lives of other victims like my mother. Until now I'd only thumbed through the books looking for bits about her, trying to find some comfort in re-reading descriptions of her life before she was killed, although this would normally be no more than a couple of lines in each book.

I was taking my first tentative steps to find other people like me.

chapter six

Sutcliffe
Resurfaces

Throughout our lives, my sisters and I have constantly been reminded that our mother was murdered by a serial killer who attracted more media attention than virtually any criminal in British history. I assumed the other victims' children would have had the same experience. I didn't want to rake up things they had put behind them, but it had been our experience that the Ripper's crimes could never be put behind you because the media would keep digging them up.

It's hard to imagine now just how big a story the hunt for the Ripper was in the 1970s. The endless headlines reflected the genuine fear that everyone felt while he was still at large and unidentified. Never again have I experienced anything close to that fear.

At the time of the arrest in 1981 the newspaper coverage became even greater. Even after the trial was all over and Sutcliffe was behind bars, the stories kept on coming. The papers just couldn't get enough of him, his wife or anyone else connected to him. I would like to have had the willpower to look away from the headlines and billboards and refuse to read any more, and perhaps some of the other victims' families have been able to do that, but something would always draw me back, even though I knew I would be newly enraged by whatever I read or heard about him.

In 2004 a new story surfaced, reporting that John Sutcliffe, the Ripper's father, was seriously ill in hospital suffering from bladder cancer, heart disease and emphysema. Apparently his son had requested to be moved to Wakefield prison so as to be near him.

This news caused a dilemma for me. On the one hand I didn't want Peter Sutcliffe to be shown any compassion whatsoever. At the same time I could see that this was unfair to his father, a man who, through no fault of his own, was now labelled as 'the Yorkshire Ripper's father'. I wouldn't have wanted to be punished for any crimes my father might have committed. I'd heard it had been a few years since they'd seen one another and I could understand that John Sutcliffe had a right to see his murdering son one last time. For all I knew he might have had a few last words he wanted to say to him.

A few weeks later John Sutcliffe died. On hearing the news I spent some time trying to put myself in his unfortunate shoes. I wondered how he must have felt, knowing he'd brought this monster into the world, a man who'd caused so much distress, suffering and pain to all those whose lives he touched. I had no way of knowing how the other victims' families had been affected but, based on my own pain and that of my sisters, I guessed the damage was probably more far reaching than I would ever know. Mothers, husbands, brothers, sisters, aunts, uncles, nieces and nephews would be involved. The actions of the Ripper would shape all our families for generations. Maybe it would only be fifty or a hundred years in the future that our connections to Peter Sutcliffe would finally dissipate. How had poor John Sutcliffe felt, knowing his son had caused all that misery?

Once his father had died, Peter Sutcliffe was placed on suicide watch. I doubted he would take his own life since it would mean he would have to meet his maker. Sutcliffe's defence had been that he'd heard voices from God, who had instructed him to clear the streets of all prostitutes. I read in one of the many books on the subject that a prostitute had once approached him and taunted him in some way. It was suggested that this was one of the reasons he later went on his murderous campaign.

Part of me thought the world would be well rid of him if he did kill himself, and that we should let God be his judge. The other part thought that he shouldn't be allowed to take an easy way out and should be made to suffer in prison for many years to come.

With Fathers' Day approaching I asked Dad if he fancied going for a meal. I still remained hopeful that somehow we would be able to build a relationship of mutual respect now that we had both got our feelings out into the open. If I could just feel that he was truly sorry for what he'd done to us as children, maybe we could move forward from there.

He agreed and we arranged to go to an Indian restaurant in Leeds. Once again I picked him up from his flat. While we were sitting in the waiting area of the restaurant Dad spotted some-one he knew at a nearby table. He waved. The waiter took us to our table after we'd ordered our drinks and we found ourselves next to the same couple.

I now felt uncomfortable, knowing I wouldn't be able to speak as openly as I wanted. We ordered our food and the conversation became a little superficial. Once the couple had left, however, I steered it around to the specific things I'd writ-ten about in the book. Dad wasn't happy.

'Some people in my family have offered me money to take you to court,' he warned.

This threat made me livid and I wasn't able to hide it.

'I know I can't sue you for telling the truth,' he said quickly, to calm me down.

As we continued to eat I brought up his physical violence towards Pauline.

'You never saw me actually hit Pauline,' he said.

I told him I did and he pounced on me.

'You're a liar. If you were in court they'd rip you to pieces with that lie.'

He was turning into the arrogant sod that he always became when he'd had a drink, the one who was always right and would try to manipulate every conversation to prove it. I racked my memory to think what it was I actually did remember from those terrible times.

'OK,' I admitted, 'I may never have actually seen you hit Pauline. But I know you did because I heard it happen so many times from our bedroom.'

'Remember that time Pauline fled the house with a broken rib and had to crawl on her hands and knees through the night?' I asked.

'I only hit her the once with the soft side of my foot,' he complained, as if tired of being falsely accused.

'You're talking bollocks. I don't have to argue with you here because when you pass away and meet your maker you'll be made to see what you've done and then you'll know how wrong you were.'

I could remember hearing him giving out long beatings through the flimsy walls of our house. They often sounded like a mixture of blows and kicks, lasting for minutes on end. Sometimes I'd had to yell out 'Daaaaaaaaaad' at the top of my voice to get him to stop.

When I tried to explain what damage he'd caused, he scoffed that it all sounded 'textbook'.

'It is textbook,' I agreed, 'because so many people have suffered at the hands of people like you. That's why they need to do so much research and produce so many studies on how to make children safe in the home.'

He had no idea what I was talking about and things were becoming a little heated between us.

'Why don't you just take a swing at me and get it over with?' he snapped.

This was so typical of him and although there were times when I'd wanted to kill him after he'd beaten my sisters, I would never have lowered myself to doing something as stupid as throwing a punch at him. He'd spoilt the meal with his attempts to undermine me and now he was resorting to violence to sort out our differences. How pathetic. I angrily shovelled my food in. Now the atmosphere was sour. Dad just wasn't the person I wanted him to be.

But as we finished our meals, the anger in me died away. We made our way out of the restaurant and back to the car. Driving to his flat, I reminded him it was now only a matter of weeks before my book was out.

'It's warts and all, Dad,' I said. I didn't want him to be able to say I hadn't warned him.

'I'm not listening to all the family who say what you're doing isn't right,' he said.

Before he got out of the car I showed him the front cover of the book, which the publishers had sent through.

'It looks OK,' he said, but I could tell he was pissed off. Actually seeing the cover finally confirmed it was true and was going to happen. I wondered if, until that moment, he'd thought I was bluffing. He got out of the car and I drove home to bed.

I was woken again about 1 a.m. by the phone. It was Dad, who had obviously been drinking in the flat after I left him.

'I've been thinking about the title of the book since I left you,' he slurred. 'You're always going to be just a boy to me, you know.'

'Is that all you rang to say?' I asked, angry at being woken.

'I don't care if you give me a hard time,' he joked. 'I don't care if we argue, as long as we keep in touch.'

I knew somewhere in there he did want to have a relationship with his son, but I didn't want to sit on the phone with him all night after having spent most of the evening arguing. Maybe he did have regrets, but I doubted if he could actually change. He didn't know how to do things any differently.

'Dad,' I said, adopting as affectionate a tone as I could manage, 'don't take this the wrong way but it's one in the morning, so I'm going to have to ask you to fuck off.'

'I know, I know,' he replied with a chuckle and put the phone down, just as I did. It had been a demanding evening and I was glad finally to be able to close my eyes.

Seeing Dad reminded me that nothing had really changed in our family. I knew that if I didn't do anything positive about my life, then the book's publication would come and go, the dust would settle and it would all be forgotten.

I decided I no longer wanted to work in the rag trade. I'd been involved in it one way or another for over ten years and, although it had been a challenge and at times I had enjoyed it, I wasn't finding it rewarding any more. I'd been lucky to be able to get into it when I did, and now I was lucky again to be offered a chance to move on. I'd been a Samaritan for eight months and the work gave me a sense of satisfaction I hadn't experienced before. I decided to take a leap of faith about my future and hand in my notice.

There was another reason why I wanted to get out as soon as possible. Any day now my life story, complete with all my mistakes, would be laid bare to everyone who knew me. I'd never told my employers about my prison record and I thought there was a strong chance they would hold it against me. I'd been getting pretty stressed about the whole thing. Laying my cards on the table in such a public way was something I knew would affect me if I were to remain at the same place of work.

I handed my notice in to Lee, the manager, who had become a good friend. He said he was happy for me that I'd found a new direction in my life, and sorry I wasn't going to stay.

As the countdown began to the day when my period of notice would be up, I started making enquiries into what type of job I was going to do next. I wanted to work in a position where I could help someone, do something worthwhile, rather than a job where the only purpose was to earn someone a profit. I made a few applications but as I had no qualifications I was finding it difficult even to get an interview. I managed to get one for a job working with people with mental health issues, but I wasn't offered the job.

Two days before I was finally due to leave the clothing company, I got a telephone call from Olga, my ex-girlfriend. She was ringing from Safeway in her hometown.

'I've just seen your book on the shelves,' she squeaked excitedly, 'alongside Jordan!'

It was 1 July, Mum's birthday, I was thrilled that Safeway had made a mistake. The publication date had been moved to 15 July but somehow the book had found its way onto the shelves early. I felt as though Mum was in some way sending her blessing.

Now all I had to worry about was whether anyone would buy it and, if they did, how they would react to my confessions. I suddenly felt very vulnerable indeed. But deep down I knew that I'd already suffered the worst when Mum was murdered all those years ago. Nothing would ever be as bad as that.

chapter seven

Party Time

I organised a party at Radisson's in Leeds to celebrate the book's publication. It was a great success. Around a hundred guests turned up, including my sisters, Sonia, Angela and Cheryl, and Pauline, who said at the end of the night how proud she was of me. She knew only too well what we'd been through because she witnessed most of it and was on the receiving end of Dad's fury many times herself.

Sandra, who had counselled me for a few years, was also there. She and Sonia had a chat and seemed to get on, so I decided that once things quietened down I'd take Sonia to see her professionally.

After the party was over, some of us went down to the local salsa club and danced away the last few hours of the night. We finally dispersed and I was just getting a taxi to go home when my phone rang. It was Rachel, one of my salsa friends.

'Your sister, Sonia, is in a little trouble,' she said. 'She's collapsed.'

I ran back to the club, my heart in my throat once again, and found Sonia laid on her back outside the club, more drunk than I'd seen her in some time. I was very angry with her. It had been a brilliant night until then. I loaded her into a taxi and made sure she got home, but yet again I was reminded that just publishing a book wasn't going to solve the problems in our family. They went back too far and were too deeply rooted to be fixed that easily.

To promote the book I travelled down to London to appear on national morning television. I arrived the day before the show and while I was in the city I met up with Jenny, an ex-girlfriend. I'd been dating her when I went into prison and she had since moved down to London. We went out to a jazz club. Afterwards we parted and I got a taxi back to my hotel where I rang Dad. I knew that from the moment I appeared on national television the next day there would be no turning back, that our family history would be public property. I was extremely anxious about how he would react when it became a reality and I wanted to let him know what was happening, so he wouldn't feel I'd gone behind his back. I might hate many of the things he'd done, but he was still my father and if I could keep the relationship going I would.

When I made the call I didn't intend to get angry with him, but he said something in his sarcastic voice that unsettled me. I started shouting at him and ended up slamming down the phone. I'd had a few to drink, too, so I can't remember much about what was said; I just know I was telling him how much of a bastard he was. I guess I felt under pressure, knowing that once I'd appeared on television the next morning the whole world would know everything about me. I had been bottling up my anger and nerves up to that point and they just exploded. The reality of the situation, of what he'd done, of what we'd been through, and of what we had lost, came out in a torrent of abuse. Maybe the anger should have been directed at someone else; the man who killed Mum. Perhaps I was using Dad as a scapegoat because he'd done some wrong. Whatever the reasons, I let rip.

I find I often get angrier than I should, just like Dad, and Sonia when she's drunk. It's always been a problem and I guess it's because I bottle up too much emotionally. When I was young I sometimes felt as though I was dissociating myself from the truth of what had happened in order to carry on. If I caught a glimpse of what had really happened I would push it away quickly. Then, over the years, when I was alone, maybe watching a TV programme, I'd burst into tears. It didn't have to be a sad programme. It could be *Blue Peter*. The sobbing would start and I would immediately nip it in the bud, knowing it wasn't normal and forcing myself to keep it under control. The problem was that the feelings of hurt and loss inside me needed to be released. That was the only way I was ever going to move on. I needed to mourn the death of my mother, which I hadn't been allowed to as a child; as a young adult, I'd pushed the feelings away as soon as I felt them. Telling the story had started the grieving process properly. Now I had to work out what to do next.

Throughout most of the television and radio interviews over the following days I avoided going into detail about the things Dad had done. In some strange way I felt I had a duty to protect him from the public, even though I'd written everything in the book. When people read a book they somehow get events into a better context, so to blurt out some of the things that had happened as isolated incidents would give them the wrong emphasis. I didn't want people to rush out and buy the book just to read about Dad drowning the family dog, because it was just one small illustration of how our lives had been for years on end.

* * *

Once I'd done all that I needed to do in London I headed back to Leeds, feeling as though I was travelling back towards a pile of hassle and grief from the family. Meeting famous presenters and being the centre of attention in a television studio was already starting to seem like a dream now that I was heading back to reality. Part of me just wanted to stay in London and avoid the whole thing, but I knew I had to face up to what I'd done. If they all hated the book and were angry with me for writing it, I would just have to cope with it.

When I got home my answering machine was full of messages. Plucking up my courage, I pressed play. I needn't have worried. They were all supportive and there was nothing from Dad.

One of the interviews I'd recorded in London was to be screened on the local Yorkshire channel, which would mean far more people in the Leeds area would get to hear about it. That night I went to bed feeling as though I was entering a new, unknown world.

Dad rang late. As usual, he'd been drinking.

'Donna's gone to the press with her story,' he told me. 'It's going to be in the *Yorkshire Post* tomorrow.'

I couldn't believe it. I knew she'd threatened to do something like this when she first heard about the book, but I'd never imagined she would actually do it.

'I'm going to screw you up,' she'd told me on that occasion, but I'd assumed that once she'd read the book and realised there was hardly anything about her in it, her mind would be put at rest.

Dad could tell I was annoyed. 'I told you this would happen,' he gloated.

'What's the story about?' I asked, genuinely puzzled as to what she would have to talk about.

'You'll have to read it yourself,' he taunted.

He and Donna had become closer over the last year and I imagined it was because Dad knew Donna was against me writing the book, which made it appear as though she was on his side. She seemed to agree with him that family secrets should stay in the family, exactly the sort of attitude I thought caused so many problems.

'I've been told a picture of you all as children was shown while you were being interviewed by Philip Schofield and Fern Britton,' he said, stumbling over his words. 'Pauline was in it. Why did you have to involve her in all this?'

I started to answer but he didn't want to listen.

'Fuck off,' he snarled, slamming down the phone.

I haven't heard from him since.

* * *

My initial reason for writing the book had been both to help Sonia and vindicate my mother, as well as to exorcise some long-term demons. I didn't want to hide my past for the rest of my life and although I knew Dad was bound to be unhappy about people knowing what he'd done, I'd felt that what I was doing was a positive thing, on balance. But why was Donna so angry? As I tried to sleep that night I suddenly wasn't so sure about the whole thing.

The next day I purchased the *Yorkshire Evening Post* and was nearly sick when I saw the story. The headline read: 'HOW DARE HE?' The more I read the more livid I became. Donna had done everything she could to discredit me and defend Dad. She'd told the reporter that Pauline's children hadn't known we weren't full brothers and sisters and now, because I'd written the book, they'd found out. Pauline had four children and the two oldest had known for years. It didn't matter to me or them that we had different mothers. The youngest hadn't known till the article appeared, it is true, but they both took the news well and the youngest assured me that as far as she was concerned I was 'still her brother'.

Donna went on to say that the book was an infringement of her privacy, although the only thing she had actually read at that point was the first draft of chapter one, which was about the time when we were all tiny children. If she'd got hold of a copy of the finished book she would have discovered she was hardly mentioned after that.

The book was about me and, to some degree, Sonia. I'd known how Donna would react if I wrote about her so I'd deliberately omitted her from the story, but if I was honest there wasn't much I could say anyway. And although she was claiming my book was an infringement of her privacy, a huge photograph of herself appeared alongside the *Yorkshire Post* article. She said she was going to sue me and contact the Home Office to contest the current privacy laws. She finished her story by saying that for every bad thing Dad had done there were twenty good things. I would have been interested to see that list!

I was soon to discover that once an article has been printed, other media use it as background information for whatever they write. When I went on BBC Leeds for an interview the same week they surprised me by asking about Donna. I humoured the presenter and sidestepped the question. I didn't want to add any more fuel to the fire. I realised I had to accept that the media would want to explore anything to do with the story, and any family feuds they could stir up would make great listening. A few weeks after coming out in Britain, the book was published in New Zealand and I was interviewed by New Zealand Radio. Even they asked why Donna was unhappy about me writing the book. I told them I didn't want to speak about it on the radio, that it was something for me and her to sort out.

The problem was I wasn't sure how we were going to sort it out since we so fundamentally disagreed about what was the right thing to do. The more I found out about how I and the other girls truly felt about things, the deeper the damage seemed to be. By speaking out and trying to move on I'd stirred up a hornets' nest of suppressed feelings. The battle to make something better of our family life was only just beginning.

chapter eight

The Next Stage

Now that I was getting a better idea of who I was and what I wanted to accomplish, I had to work out how I was going to do it. Was I kidding myself to think that I could achieve anything more? How could I find out?

I already knew that having no educational qualifications meant I was going to struggle to get the sorts of jobs that I wanted, but I had to start somewhere. I contacted an organisation that helped people get work in support roles of one type or another. It had been my experience with finding previous jobs, and in getting the book published, that perseverance was everything. If you just went out looking for what you wanted and didn't give up until you had found it, you would eventually succeed.

The staff at the organisation told me I would have to go on

weekly preparation classes before I could be given a work place-
ment. I knew this meant I would be starting at the very bottom
of the ladder in the line of work I was interested in, but I had no
choice. At least I would be starting. I was going to have to work
for years before I got anywhere and the pay was terrible, but
I had a foot on the right ladder.

Although I registered for the organisation's next 'intake' I
wasn't completely sure whether there were any better avenues
I could be taking. I didn't have anyone to turn to for advice but
somehow I felt as though it would all turn out for the best.
I hadn't known who to talk to about publishing a book either,
but I'd managed to find the right people.

Things had to work out because I'd resigned from a job,
which paid reasonably well, and the advance for the book
wouldn't last for ever. Although I did occasionally feel twinges
of panic, I felt that if Mum was 'up there' watching over me she
would guide me. I had to hold onto my belief in myself. If I
didn't believe I could achieve more, then who else would?

Sonia, meanwhile, needed practical help. I made an appointment for her to visit Sandra, my ex-counsellor. I picked her up
and drove the thirty miles to Sandra's address, waiting outside
while she had her first session. Sandra had helped me with a lot

of the things that had happened to me as a child and some of the things about my adult life that I was unhappy about. I was sure Sonia would benefit from the same sort of help. I felt optimistic as I sat in the car.

Once the session was over Sonia got back into the passenger seat and we set off towards her house.

'Do you think this is going to work?' I asked cautiously, not wanting to put any pressure on her.

'I'm not sure yet.'

She was right. It was only her first session after all and I'd spent three years with Sandra, seeing her every three weeks. I didn't ask any more, leaving her with her thoughts.

I dropped Sonia off at her house, hoping she would not drink before her next session in two weeks' time. Even as I wished it I knew I was hoping for a miracle and, as expected, she was drinking again the next day.

Media interest in my story was continuing to build and I was contacted by a number of television companies about the possibility of making a documentary. I didn't want to be involved in something just for the sake of it so I turned most of them down, but eventually I decided a documentary might be a good vehicle for contacting the other families who lost their mothers to

Sutcliffe. Far more people watched television programmes than read books, and if they could see Sonia and me and hear us talking, they would hopefully realise we were sincere.

I chose to work with a company based in Leeds who had made programmes about Sutcliffe before. I thought that as well as using the company to help me meet the other families, I could also tap into their contacts and maybe find out more about the man who had so changed my life. I finally agreed to go ahead with the film, provided one of the other themes of the programme would be to look into how Mum became labelled as a prostitute. If it was untrue, as everyone who knew her assured me it was, I felt I had a duty to her to ask questions about it and I could use the documentary to set the record straight. At the very least I wanted to show her as more than a victim of Sutcliffe, as a loving mother with a history and a right to live, someone who is still sorely missed every day. It was now the late summer of 2004 and filming wasn't due to begin until January 2005, so I had plenty of time to think about what it was I was trying to achieve.

Two weeks later, when I went to collect Sonia to take her to her next counselling session with Sandra, she wouldn't answer the door. I knew she had to be in the house because I could see the key in the door on the other side. I called her mobile number but the phone was switched off. Then I drove round the corner to Angela's house. It was possible she had locked herself out and gone there. Angela said Sonia had been there earlier but warned me that she'd been drinking.

I couldn't believe Sonia would do this, but then I wasn't an alcoholic. I didn't think like one and I wouldn't understand how Sonia needed a drink to deal with the pressure of talking about her feelings to Sandra. I felt let down but I also felt as though I'd let Sandra down, too. I rang her and explained what had happened. She was great about it, telling me not to worry and that this kind of thing was to be expected. We made arrangements to go back the following week.

I drove home, my heart aching.

Letters from readers of my book were arriving almost daily. They were all moving and heart-warming. People told me how much they'd enjoyed it, although many admitted that 'enjoy' was the wrong word. A lot of them had also had to deal with murder within their own families and found they could relate to my story, often mentioning the way in which people refused to talk about murder because there was such a stigma attached to it. Perhaps they were relieved to be able to write to me because

I could understand something of their experience. It's one thing to watch a murder in a film or television drama, but these fictions never show the reality of what murder does to a victim's relatives, and how family life is slaughtered.

Actually coming face-to-face with someone who has lost a loved one through murder or manslaughter can be too uncomfortable for most people to handle. But those of us who have lost a family member in this way often want to talk about our loved ones. Even calling Mum a 'loved one' seems to be selling her short somehow. She was the woman who carried me for nine months, whose body I emerged from, who fed and clothed me and loved me unconditionally. That's who I lost and it's why I still ache to be close to her again.

We want to feel the love we still have for those who have had their lives cut short, and keep it alive. We want to remember them. Brushing it under the carpet, as happened to my sisters and I when we were children, is the last thing we want, and many experts would argue that it does far more harm than good. Maybe if I'd been able to talk to someone about what had happened to Mum and to us as children, I might have been better able to deal with life when I grew up. I felt as though I was in a straitjacket as a child, not being allowed to talk about Mum. I wanted to break free of that straitjacket and talk about her and about how I was feeling, about what was going on inside my young mind. Even now, the response to *Just a Boy* from some of the McCanns in Leeds made me feel as though they were still trying to apply the straitjacket. I had to find a way of leaving those ties behind if I wanted to move on.

Some of the letters I received came from countries as far afield as Australia, Brazil, France, Germany, Gibraltar, New Zealand, Spain and Uganda, and told stories which shocked me deeply.

A lady called Pam from Uganda wrote to tell me how her father was taken away by soldiers for political reasons in 1984, when she was six years old. She remembers how he gave her a short ride on his motorbike that very day. It is the only memory she has of him. She explained:

We have had different tales about his death. Some say he was roasted to death, others that he was fed to the crocodiles. Others say he was chopped up. Sometimes I imagine I will meet him on the streets, walking lame or something. I never stop thinking about him. My mum died later in 1993 and she left eight of us and, like you, we had a very troubled upbringing, my uncle raping my sister, my elder brothers escaping from school to join the army in Rwanda ...

She thought that copies of *Just a Boy* should be distributed to children living in camps in northern Uganda: 'Children who are forced to kill their brothers and sisters, forced to live by the gun and drugs and rape, children whose innocence has been taken, stolen and shattered.' I decided I would send her some copies of the book. Amazingly Pam had managed to get herself accepted at Leeds University but didn't receive the scholarship she had hoped for and so was unable to take up the offer.

Letters like this brought home to me just how many people in the world are suffering, that in some countries stories like mine and Sonia's were commonplace. They made me even more determined to try to help people in some small way.

Another lady, Rachel Lavender, wrote to tell me how her father was killed by a hit-and-run driver who had managed to repair his car by the time the police got to him, then how her mother and aunts were killed by a man who set fire to the cottage they were all sleeping in on an island off the west coast of Ireland. Rachel had been working in the probation service already when her mother and aunts were killed and had planned to become a probation officer, but for a while after the tragedy she couldn't bring herself to work with offenders. 'Eventually I decided to go back,' she told me. 'Why should the individual who took away so much from me take my career as well?'

I also heard from the founder of Samaritans, who'd read an article about my story in *The Times* and was pleased, and not at all surprised, to hear that I'd become a Samaritan. I heard from police officers, prison officers, doctors, teachers and many other professionals, all saying they now had a better insight into the way a child's mind is affected by major trauma.

Most of the letters came from people who'd personally suffered child abuse, domestic abuse, violence, loss and trauma of one shape or another. They told me they'd felt inspired after reading *Just a Boy* as it showed them it was possible to emerge from a hard life and be able to tell the story. Teenagers also told me they'd learned a lot of life's lessons through my book, taking in warnings about abuse, drugs, alcohol and the dangers awaiting them in the wider world. I'd never expected so many passionate reactions. These letters were further confirmation for me that it had been the right decision to tell the whole truth.

I wondered if Dad would ever know how far the story of his actions had spread and how he would feel about it if he did know. In telling my story I had wanted to interrupt the violence I had seemed to inherit. Only when the truth is faced by someone does it then have to be faced by others, even if they deny it.

* * *

When the next appointment for Sonia to see Sandra came round, she was in a fit state to go. I told her how disappointed I'd been in her behaviour on the previous occasion.

'Stop going on about it,' was her reply, so I did.

At the end of the session she admitted it had gone better than the first and she was now looking forward to the next one. I hoped we'd turned a corner and that she wouldn't let me down again.

But the next time I went to pick her up she wasn't even in the house and once again her mobile phone was switched off. It was hopeless. I realised this wasn't going to work and I couldn't keep letting Sandra down. Just as I thought we were starting to make some progress we seemed to be back at square one. Many people had told me over the years that an alcoholic will never stop drinking until they're ready, and I knew now that no amount of pleading from me would bring my sister to her senses. I would just have to wait until she decided the time was right.

One reader's letter was from someone I vaguely knew. Caroline used to be married to a cousin on Dad's side of the family, although they had split up around fifteen years ago. She told me she was very moved by the book and was desperately sorry she hadn't paid more attention to me as a young boy. I hadn't come into contact with her that often, but I did remember seeing her at the house of Aunty Anne, Dad's sister.

Caroline explained how she had tried to ask us about how we were getting on a few times after Mum died, but was told that it was better not to bring the subject up, in case it upset the children, as if not mentioning it would mean the problem ceased to exist.

Caroline had felt particularly moved by my story because of her personal connection to me and my family, but also because she was now working with children who were troubled, traumatised and whose lives had been dramatically altered by loss and by experiences of abuse and neglect. She told me that if I ever needed any help with anything I should drop her a line. I phoned her immediately and left a message. She called back the same evening, full of praise for the book and regret at not trusting herself to come and talk to me all those years earlier.

'They told me your dad and Pauline were doing a great job of bringing you up on their own,' she said.

I daresay Dad had done a good job convincing the rest of the family that everything was fine and, since we were not allowed to talk about our feelings, they would never have heard anything different from any of us.

'So,' she said after we'd been talking for a while, 'what are you doing with yourself now the book is done?'

I explained that I was giving a lot of thought to what I wanted to do with my life and that it would hopefully involve caring for others. She seemed to be interested in helping and invited me to her home to meet her new husband, Mike, who is a doctor. They made me feel very welcome, opening a bottle of champagne to celebrate my achievements so far. Both seemed to be from a different world to the one I'd been brought up in, and the one where Dad still resided, and yet they both came from working-class backgrounds. It wasn't just the material differences. They were interested in the world and people around them; they wanted to help others and to make their lives better. They believed that it was possible to change the way things were. In the world I had come from no one seemed to see any hope of improving things for themselves or for anyone else.

She convinced me that, given my achievement in writing the book, my resilience and my capacity for reflective thinking, I would be well placed to progress into higher education. Caroline told me how when she left Ireland twenty-five years ago, with virtually no qualifications, she gradually found her way into higher education. She was now Head of Child and Adolescent Psychotherapy at a Leeds teaching hospital and was also a university lecturer. She impressed upon me the idea that I had an intellectual capacity and emotional intelligence and that I could certainly further develop my talents. She helped me to think about my next step, suggesting we meet up with a past colleague and longstanding friend of hers, now retired from Bradford University, Eileen Moxon.

Some weeks later Caroline drove me to meet Eileen. In spite of my nerves I was determined to go through with it, and was keen to pick as many brains as possible. Caroline's words had set me thinking. Writing the book was just the start of understanding my life. If there was any way I could follow in Caroline's footsteps then I would like to try. I would love to become the sort of person that a child in the position I had once been in could turn to. Caroline had found a way to become just that kind of person and I could think of nothing better to aim for.

Eileen lived in one of the more exclusive areas in Leeds in a massive detached house. Here I was, a young man with no qualifications, standing on the doorstep of a retired university Head of Department (and ex-councillor). For a while I just wanted to run back to the safety of my little home.

Once we were inside, Eileen's husband, Paul, brought in tea on a tray with a teapot and jug of milk, which helped settle my nerves. I gave Eileen a copy of my book.

'I'll read it tonight,' she promised, 'and give you my honest opinion as soon as I can.'

I believed her.

We met again the following day.

'I think you should get the education you missed out on all those years ago,' she said, bluntly. 'You've been given this opportunity because of the money from the book and you should grab it with both hands. You should go to university.'

One of Caroline's memories from reading *Just a Boy* was the image of me, at times of great distress and depression, looking out at the Leeds University tower. She thought it was significant that this tower featured so prominently since I was a boy looking for a way to understand his mother's death. She could also detect that I was still searching for meaning and that I had a huge appetite for knowledge, which I could satiate through higher education. She hoped I could go to the university that seemed so out of reach to me as a child.

University was an option I'd never even considered, coming from a council estate where hardly anyone went on to further education. I could see now that never having taken my exams when I was sixteen was a big mistake, but at the time my priority was to get out of the house, away from Dad's aggression, and start working in order to be independent. It is a trap many working-class boys fall into, finding themselves dependent on employers instead of family.

Eileen also thought that it might be a bit soon for me to be working in a job in which I was supporting damaged people, since things had really only just started to change for me. I realised she was right. I knew I'd started to heal, but there was still a lot of work to do. Eileen must have been able to see I still had some way to go in my recovery and that a few years of education would give me the confidence I lacked.

The idea certainly appealed to me, but I didn't believe there was any way I would be able to get in, not having any of the entrance qualifications. As far as I was concerned, university was for middle-class families, where the parents were in a position to fund their kids while they studied. I couldn't believe it would ever happen, but I could see no harm in at least enquiring.

I spent hours that night hunched over my computer researching universities and colleges in the area. I thought more about the white tower of Leeds University and how it had played a symbolic part in my life, being the biggest landmark I could see from my bedroom in the house where we had lived with Mum. It could also be seen from Beckett's Park Children's Home and from the house we shared with Dad. I would stare at it for hours on end after Mum's death, and even today, whenever I drive into Leeds city centre, I feel drawn to it. It was one of the few constant things in my childhood.

When the coordinator at the university wrote at the end of August to ask me in for an informal chat I could hardly believe it. As I walked towards the tower with a copy of my book in my hand, I hoped there might just be a slim possibility I could get in. I'd heard how students would often struggle to achieve the necessary marks to gain entrance to such a well-respected university. I walked through the university grounds smiling to myself. None of the few students I passed would have any idea of the significance of that tower to me.

I headed towards the Social Science department, growing more nervous as I approached. I entered the building and headed for the second floor. For a moment I fantasised about being a student, thinking how, as far as anyone who saw me that sunny afternoon was concerned, I could already be one. I knew this day could be a significant turning point in my life.

I also realised that if I was successful I would have years of study ahead of me, and right then I had no idea how I was going to fund it. I prayed Mum was looking down and that she would guide me through it. I knocked at the door of the office of the course coordinator.

She invited me in and immediately put me at my ease, breaking down all the barriers I'd imagined there would be between us. Sitting in her office, I talked about my decision to change career. I didn't go into detail about the book, simply explaining it was about a troubled childhood.

She told me that they were starting a pilot degree course

called an Extended Degree and that it was to be a four-year degree with the equivalent of a foundation year in Social Science followed by the degree of choice afterwards. She thought this might well be the way forward for me.

It sounded like a long journey but I immediately knew it could be my path to the sort of future I wanted. If I could complete the degree I could even do a conversion to psychology afterwards, which interested me. I didn't know how I was going to afford it, but perhaps a way would present itself. However, in order to get on the programme I first had to prove that my English and Maths were up to scratch.

A week later I came back to take the entrance exam in the same office. The maths I found easy, always having enjoyed working with numbers, and the English question was about the Welfare State. I had to read an article and then re-write it in my own words with my own title. I called it 'The Well-fair State?' There were a lot of words in the article I didn't understand but I grasped the key points. The coordinator marked the maths paper while I was there, telling me I had scored 97 per cent. She said she would let me know about the English in a day or so.

I was nervous, believing that if I failed the dream would be over, but I passed with no problem and was accepted. I was over the moon. The first hurdle was overcome and I was on my way. I couldn't ring Mum, or Dad for that matter, to tell them how pleased I was, but I was determined now to go though with it, even if it meant I had to sell my house to fund the degree. I'd seen where I wanted to go and I wasn't going to let anything stand in my way.

I then had to apply officially, but was told there was no reason I shouldn't start at the end of September. It seemed I might be able to allow myself to have a dream with a reasonable hope of making it a reality.

I wanted to get the education in order to be able to follow in similar footsteps to Caroline, and help others, especially children. I'd heard from so many people that there was a lack of help for individuals in the world. I knew that I could look myself in the mirror and be sure that my intentions were good. Dad and some of his family would never see that, believing maybe that it was all about making money out of Mum's death, but I knew, and those close to me knew, that this couldn't have been further from the truth. I was on a lifelong journey to undo the damage that had been done to me in order to be able to help others.

chapter nine

Back to School

One night, before my university term started, I was enjoying myself at my salsa club, mixing and dancing with friends, when I noticed that two cousins from Dad's side of the family had walked in. Simon I had always got on with, but his sister, Divina, I didn't know very well. Simon said hello and told me he didn't have a problem with me writing the book. He chatted about his own childhood for a while, admitting it hadn't been a bed of roses. But when Divina noticed me she put both her hands up in front of her face and made a cross with her forefingers, as if protecting herself from the devil.

It seemed she was another member of my family who was in some sort of denial about what had happened. Shouldn't she have been doing this to my father? It was as if they could excuse him for what he did, but not me for talking about it. Her husband was with her and told me not to worry about it.

But Divina's reaction upset my night. I didn't want to think what the rest of Dad's family were saying about me. I left the club early and went home.

I soon learned she wasn't the only one who disapproved of what I'd done. My father had beaten his wife, his girlfriend and his children and he had been forgiven. My crime was to write about it. Ever since the disastrous Fathers' Day meal, when Dad told me the family in Ireland had offered him money to sue me for writing the book, it felt as if the McCann clan had turned their backs on me. They thought that I was the one who had behaved badly, not him. I even considered changing my name to Newlands, since my mother's side of the family seemed happy with what I had done and continued to encourage me. Mum and Dad had been separated anyway at the time of her death, and would have divorced, so it didn't seem unreasonable that I or my sisters might have taken her name rather than his. It also occurred to me that if I were ever to have children I would be able to shield them from the history of the McCann name and its association with the Ripper by taking a different name.

But I just had to accept that I would have to live with the McCanns' disapproval since I could do nothing about changing their minds. I'd put my side of things as clearly as I could in the book; if they still disagreed with me there was little more I could add. I was going to have to be philosophical about it.

When you've suffered a trauma like a murder in the family, I think it makes you more sensitive to stories of other people's troubles. I watched in dismay when reports started to appear on the news of rebels taking as many as a thousand children and parents hostage in a school in Chechnya. When it was reported a few days later that armed soldiers were storming the building. I dropped to my knees in front of the television, fearing I was about to witness a bloodbath but not able to bring myself to turn the set off.

'No!' I yelled as I watched the naked, distressed children fleeing for their lives to the sound of gunfire. I could imagine the panic and confusion and fear they must be feeling. I dreaded to think what sights they had witnessed inside the school.

Seeing the crowds of parents waiting anxiously outside the building for their children to come running out, thoughts flashed through my mind of how many families in that town were going to be suffering in the way only someone who has been through something similar can understand. To witness the mothers and fathers weeping for their children filled me with an overwhelming sadness and I walked round and round the house, willing the whole thing to end, hardly able to bear the rawness of my own emotions.

The horror went on for hours and the final death count rose into the hundreds as the reluctant authorities eventually released news of explosions inside the school hall. Today's society is very different to the one I was brought up in during the 1970s, but I was struck by how the current fear of terrorists is similar to the terror that was felt by the people of Yorkshire during the Ripper's murderous campaign.

My first day at university arrived. I couldn't wait to get there. I'd loved being at school, and had always been in the top stream, willing to put my hand up if I didn't understand something. It felt so good now to be able to tell people who asked what I was doing that I was at Leeds University. I was proud as Punch as I walked from the city centre towards the white tower, watching it grow taller as I approached.

I entered the class feeling quite nervous. We were taken to enrol in one of the large halls, joining queues of hundreds upon hundreds of people, mostly aged between eighteen and twenty-one, a lot younger than my thirty-four years. Standing amongst them, I wondered whether any of them had any idea what kind of background I had. I doubted it.

We were told what we were going to be covering during the year and it all sounded so different from anything I had ever known. Would Dad have been interested in the origins of conservatism, liberalism, Marxism, the Welfare State, feminism, law and criminality? I doubted that, too. 'Textbook', he would have called it, derisively.

I soon found out that 'textbook' was exactly what it was. We were given reading lists each week and had to attend talks on disability, race and ethnicity. Although it was all alien to me, I was hungry to learn new things. I wanted desperately to know more about the world in which we lived and how it had been shaped.

At first I panicked at the amount of reading we were expected to do, until I learned how to speed- and skim-read, concentrating only on what I needed to know. Suddenly I began to feel I actually could do it. I had so much to learn – at first, I didn't even know the difference between being 'objective' and 'subjective' – and realised that the academic world was vast. I listened avidly to guest speakers such as Colin Barnes, a well-respected author of many books on disability, who, I discovered, had succeeded in changing the way in which disabled people were seen in Britain. I also remember a talk by an ex-social worker, and another lecture on ethnicity in Britain, which made me think much more deeply about society. When one of the tutors brought in a video about why West Indians first came to England, it was the first time I'd realised that they had been invited here. We saw them arriving in their suits and ties, expecting a warm welcome, and I felt ashamed to think how they were treated, and often still are.

The class was made up of a broad range of people, most of whom had got there by unconventional means. Quite a few of us had left school without qualifications, some were single mothers and others were middle-aged. We were all of varying abilities and heading in different directions, but everyone was friendly and interested in one another.

I'd initially thought I might do a degree in social work but, after seeing a video of social workers in Bradford, I decided I would get a more general degree first and then specialise, rather than limiting my options. Many of the social workers I talked to seemed to be unhappy and found their work thankless. I asked Eileen what she thought and she agreed that being a trainee social worker would probably be difficult for me to cope with. It was often highly emotional work, dealing with difficult issues. Part of the training would have involved working with families and I had to agree that I wasn't ready for that yet. I was getting a much better appreciation of my own limits, as well as the different possibilities open to me in the future. In the end I chose the Social Policy degree because I thought it would give me the education I wanted and the academic confidence I still needed. I couldn't believe that I was actually in a position to be considering such choices.

As I wasn't working there was a strong chance that I would end the course with no money left from the publication of the book at all. I hadn't told anyone in the class about it and was surprised when one of the younger girls told me she'd read it. I then discovered that quite a few of them had read it because it dealt with so many of the issues that we would go on to study once the foundation year was complete, such as domestic violence and child abuse, child psychology and development. I heard that a student on another course had chosen my book to write a critique on. I felt so proud of my achievement. It was strange to think these people knew so much about me, but not that strange because I was used to people having read about Mum in the papers for all those years. In a way, *Just a Boy* was an extension of that same story.

When it came to writing essays I would often send my first attempts to Eileen, who assured me she was happy to give advice and mentor me through the year. I would then go to see her and she would help me phrase things in a more acceptable academic way, taking out superfluous words. I knew I was in a privileged position, getting such expert extra tuition, and I would absorb everything she taught me, putting it to use in the next piece of work

A month after starting at the university, I was in a restaurant in Sheffield that sometimes hosted salsa classes. It was a small, intimate place in a side street off one of the main roads, with low lights, a wooden floor and a Latin atmosphere to match the tapas they served. All the staff were Spanish or Latino and looked as if they were about to break into dance at any moment. I got talking to a woman who was having a meal there with some girlfriends. She was a nice enough person and sounded quite posh to me, since she had a southern accent. When I mentioned it she assured me she wasn't posh.

'I came north a few years ago,' she told me, 'to become a midwife. I only recently qualified.'

She'd been a nanny in London and had gone to an exclusive nanny school, where, she told me, the nanny for the Princesses Beatrice and Eugenie had also studied. At thirty-seven, she was a few years older than me.

We got on well and I knew we had a connection. I loved her smile and her blonde hair. She had fair skin and beautiful blue eyes. She told me her name was Helen and I felt I could see a nice, genuine, grounded person. I decided to ask her to meet up with me for a meal some other time. I was pleased when she said yes, but I wondered what it was she thought she could see in me. Here I was, after all, thirty-four years old and still trying to sort my life out. My self-confidence was very easily shaken even now.

'What do you do for a living?' she asked.

'I've just decided to return to education,' I replied. 'I'm at Leeds University.'

'How can you afford it if you don't work?'

'I've come into a small amount of money which means I can afford not to work for a while,' I said.

It wasn't really a lie, even though I knew I was giving the impression I'd inherited money. I didn't feel ready to tell her about the book and my past, and that I had no idea how I would fund the rest of the four-year course when the book advance ran out. There is only so much you can tell someone at a first meeting!

A few days later, after our first date, she invited me into her home when I dropped her off. I thought it was brave of her and wondered whether she felt as comfortable with me as I did with her. I thought we'd got on famously and didn't want the night to end. She had a lovely house and it was obvious she looked after it. I hadn't been drinking because I was driving and she'd told me she didn't really drink much.

'It's a bit of a sore subject,' she said.

'My sister is a struggling alcoholic,' I admitted.

'My mum died last year after being an alcoholic for twenty years.'

We now had something major in common and over the next weeks and months, as I continued to try and help Sonia, Helen was able to understand exactly how I was feeling. We talked and talked into the night after that first date and it felt as though I'd known her for years rather than days.

She told me she'd also lost her father two years earlier; it was obviously a difficult subject for her to talk about. He'd died eight months before his wife, and I tried to imagine how painful that must have been for Helen. Once again it felt as though we had something else in common. Although my father was alive, I knew I also had no parents I could turn to in times of need.

I soon started to feel guilty about the white lie I'd told about coming into some money. Caught up in the honesty of the conversation, I felt it would be wrong of me not to be open about my past. She would find out soon enough about Mum, Dad and the book, so it would be better if I came clean. The whole story was a major part of my life and if we were going to see one another again then she would need to know it.

'My mum was the first victim of Peter Sutcliffe,' I finally said.

She looked shocked, as though she couldn't comprehend

what I was telling her, and told me later that she'd heard the words but didn't want to accept them. We talked about what had happened on that fateful night and I also told her about some of Dad's behaviour. I explained about the book and how it was that which had helped me afford university.

I left Helen's house at four in the morning and drove home, hoping she wouldn't be put off by everything she'd now learned about me. Something told me we'd both seen things in each other which we really liked. I hoped I hadn't endangered that by moving too fast.

I needn't have worried. We started seeing each other regularly and it was soon obvious that we were both equally committed to one another. Helen showed a lot of interest in my past but I still felt I needed to limit the amount I told her. She said she wanted to wait until we'd been dating for a couple of months before she read the book. I was fine about that. I was a little worried what she would make of my time spent in prison.

After a couple of months, once I had begun to stay over at Helen's house, I would read a couple of chapters at a time to her while we lay in bed. Sometimes she would become upset and hold me tight after we had turned out the light. It was a lot for her to take in. Having had loving parents, the sort of abuse we suffered as children was completely alien to her.

As I got to know her, I was constantly impressed by the way

Helen seemed to be able to blend smoothly into any situation she found herself in. We could be visiting Angela or Sonia or sitting at a dinner party and she would be equally at ease. I've heard that we're attracted to people who have aspects to their characters that we lack, and I could see she had a tremendous confidence which I didn't. We made a good team. She was also a good organiser and started to convert me to the pleasures of eating natural food, avoiding additives and cooking everything from scratch.

There was so much about her that was good I could hardly believe she was interested in someone like me. The little boy who had once looked at his reflection in the mirror and been unable to believe anyone would ever fancy him, had to admit that someone wonderful actually found him attractive.

chapter ten

Sonia's Slide

One morning, Vicky, who used to be married to my Uncle Isaac, rang to tell me Sonia was in a terrible state again and that I'd better come round to hers quickly. She'd already had a good few drinks when Vicky had run into her the previous evening and had offered to take her for another. As so often happened, Sonia became nasty and aggressive as she grew drunker and had ended the evening by going off with some guy.

That morning she'd turned up at Vicky's house, still drunk and now crying. She was in a terrible mess. I drove over immediately and my heart sank to find my sister looking worse than I'd seen her for a long time. Normally when I turned up on occasions like this her spirits would rise a little, but not this time. After a cup of tea I got her into my car and drove her home.

'Don't worry about the last few days,' I told her, trying to calm her. 'Just have a bath and go to bed. You'll feel better after a long sleep and some food.'

I put her to bed, hoping she'd realise that she had reached rock bottom and would understand that she couldn't carry on like this. I was wrong. After a night's sleep she went out drinking again to try and dull the depression that had enveloped her on waking. She then decided to turn to the man who had caused her so much pain in the past – Dad. When she got to his flat, however, she found it empty, so she left him a note, which read: '*Dad, I need you, Sonia.*' It was a simple, desperate message from a daughter to her father, asking him to make things better. She posted it through his letterbox and stumbled home.

She never heard from him.

Despite Sonia's return to the drink, her daughter, Leanne, decided to go back to live with her. Leanne was only eighteen and it was hard for her to have to deal with a drunken, abusive mother. I was getting calls from Sonia, ranting about Leanne, but when Leanne calmly explained what was going on it was obvious Sonia's drinking was the main cause of their problems. It was one thing for me to try and help my sister but it was too much to expect her young daughter to deal with her.

'When are you going to stop all this drinking?' I asked Sonia in desperation.

'When I'm ready,' she replied.

I'd told myself this before and I knew she was right. No amount of persuasion or shouting from me was going to make any difference. All I could do was pray she would decide to stop herself soon. I knew that if she carried on like this she was going to do irreparable damage to her health. If she didn't mend her ways it would not be long before I would be attending her funeral. Sonia was the closest person in the world to me and to lose her would be unbearable.

The SAMM organisation was arranging a memorial service in Manchester Cathedral for people who'd lost loved ones through murder and manslaughter. The date was set for 29 October, the day back in 1975 when we last saw Mum alive.

Sonia can recall Mum getting ready to go out that night, but my enduring memory is of the growing realisation that Mum hadn't arrived home and that Angela, the youngest, kept crying. I remember Sonia pretending to read Angela a story to get her to fall asleep, while all the time Mum was lying dead on the field at the back of the house.

Keen to distract myself on the day and push such a painful memory to the back of my mind, I asked Sonia if she fancied taking a drive over the Pennines for the service. She jumped at the chance.

'There's no way I'm taking you if you're drinking,' I warned her.

The inducement must have worked because when I arrived to pick her up I was relieved to see she was sober. We drove over to Manchester and hoped to be able to see the cathedral from the road as we approached the city centre. We spotted it straight away and parked. I'd told Michaela that we would be there and I was pleased to see her with all her family. In the cathedral we each signed a book of remembrance and picked up a small candle. Then we took our places at the back of the packed cathedral and sat with our unlit candles. I saw another couple of friends whose relatives had also been killed. It felt like being part of a community.

It was a very moving occasion, especially when two speakers stood to read out a list of all the people to be remembered in the service. They took it in turns to read out the names and the list seemed to go on for ever. Name after name of innocent victims whose lives had been unfairly taken away, sometimes with deliberate malice, sometimes not. As each name was read out any family members for that person stood with a lit candle. There must have been at least a hundred and fifty of us. Eventually everyone was standing, as if we were making a statement for them, in their memory.

I was struggling to hold back the tears and eventually I just let them go. For those moments I felt as though I had the most direct link possible to Mum. Away from all the mundane business of the world this was our moment. The choir sang and I continued to cry. Sonia passed me a tissue from her pocket, but it was soon too drenched by my tears to be of any use.

When the choir fell silent we all extinguished our candles and sat. We then sang a song together, followed by a moving solo from a woman who sounded like an opera singer. It was simultaneously beautiful and upsetting. Once she finished I tried to pull myself together. I was reminded of the overwhelming emotion I'd felt at Grandma's funeral the previous year.

'We need to do something like that for the people of Yorkshire,' I said as we drove back from Manchester, and was determined to start looking into it as soon as possible.

chapter eleven

Turning Detective

Shortly after the memorial service I was contacted by a freelance journalist who wanted to inform me that in the coming weeks there was to be a press conference in Leeds where it would be announced that the 'copy-cat theory' – which I had learned about in the mid-1990s from a writer called Noel O'Gara, who had published a book about the Ripper case – was true. O'Gara's theory suggested that some of the Yorkshire Ripper's victims were in fact killed by someone else.

The journalist gave me details, which included a press release, letters and affidavits from a person who said he'd been working for the solicitors acting for Sutcliffe in 1981. This man claimed that one of Sutcliffe's solicitors had said that Sutcliffe had not carried out all the murders.

The press conference, orchestrated by O'Gara, was to be

attended by a local councillor and a former member of West Yorkshire Police who was apparently willing to go on record to say that 'it was known at the top echelons of West Yorkshire Police that there was not one, but two killers'.

I couldn't believe what I was reading. Had I been blaming the wrong man for Mum's death all this time? Had Noel O'Gara been right all along? Was there a police cover-up? Was it possible that Sutcliffe hadn't actually killed Mum?

Just as things were coming together in my life, a worrying cloud of confusion enveloped me. I rang Mark, the journalist who was going to chair the press conference, and asked him about everything, explaining how worried this was making me feel.

We decided we should meet up and made a date for two days' time at the scene of Mum's murder. In the meantime I read up on Sutcliffe's confession. He stated in court that he had picked Mum up on the main dual carriageway that led to our street. (The bus stop where Sonia and I waited for Mum was on the same dual carriageway.) Sutcliffe then stated that they drove into the car park where Mum died, a rectangular area with its entrance on the south side. On the north side was the Prince Phillip Nursery and on the east side was the grass embankment where Mum's body was found.

He said he drove into the car park and parked at the east side, facing the embankment, with the car lights on. I didn't see anything strange so far. Then he stated that he and Mum had walked onto the slope and that she had laid down. I just couldn't understand why she would have laid on the grass at one in the morning when her house was just fifty yards away, but I had to face up to the possibility that she might have done, having been drinking all evening.

He then said that after the murder he'd reversed all the way out of the car park in an anxious state and through the narrow entrance. There was something about this I didn't like. If Sutcliffe had parked the car the way that he said he did, facing east, then all he would have had to do was to reverse the car in a three-point turn and drive out forwards. It was almost fifty yards from where he claimed he parked his car to the entrance. The car park was big enough to turn the car very easily without having to manoeuvre it backwards in the dark through a small gap. In one of the many books on the crimes of Sutcliffe, I'd read that the caretaker of the nursery, whose house was next door to his place of work, had reported that his African Ridgeback dog had remained silent throughout the night despite the fact that one of the windows of his house was open. He'd also reported that he'd heard nothing at all, which struck him afterwards as strange.

I decided I would try to find the caretaker if he was still alive. I checked his name in one of the books I had and went through the phone directory. There were only four people with the same surname and initial as the man I was looking for. I started dialling.

I explained to the first person on my shortlist that I was looking for a couple by the same name who used to be caretakers at Prince Phillip Nursery in the 1970s. The first and second calls came to nothing but the third call was answered by an elderly man, whose name was John.

'Yes,' he said, 'I was the caretaker.'

I told him who I was and asked if I could visit him. He was retired now and said he could meet me the same afternoon. I drove over to the other side of Leeds to the address he gave me and knocked on his door. It was snowing. I hoped I would be able to get home without getting stuck in the slow traffic. The man who answered the door was in his eighties and looked like someone who had worked all his life. He invited me in and I took a seat in his small living room. He explained what had happened the morning Mum had been killed.

'I was up and around outside the bungalow doing something in the garden by about seven,' he said. 'The milkman had been delivering a crate of milk and he told me something had caught his eye in the early-morning mist. He shouted out that he'd spotted something on the grass slope. I told him I'd go and have a look.'

So John was actually the first person to find my mother dead on the embankment. I'd always thought it was the milkman but in fact it was this old man who had first realised the bundle was actually a human being. As small children we had all attended the nursery for some time so John had recognised the dead woman as Mum.

'I knew she lived on the Avenue,' he said. 'It was a shock to find her there like that. I knew she had children because I'd seen her bringing you to the nursery. I shouted for the milkman to ring the police immediately while I stayed with your mum.'

Hearing him talking about something that was so much a part of my life was a shock. I was in a daze for a few minutes as I tried to take all the facts in.

'The police soon arrived and started asking questions,' John went on. 'I wanted my wife to be spared seeing your mum on the hill, but the police didn't cover her body quick enough. She opened the living-room curtains to be greeted by that awful sight. She was traumatised by what she saw and her health started to deteriorate. She died some years after and I think it was because of the shock of what she'd witnessed.'

Once again I was made aware of the far-reaching effects of a murder. How many more secondary victims were there? So many people had been involved in the Ripper investigation that the final figure could have been into the thousands.

'What about the African Ridgeback dog you had at the time?' I asked. 'I read that it didn't hear anything through the open window. Wasn't that strange?'

'No,' John corrected me. 'They got that wrong. The dog was outside in its kennel.'

'Are you sure?' I asked.

'Absolutely. It was outside all night, only three or four yards from where your mum was found.'

This was a bombshell to me. The dog had been yards from where Sutcliffe had said he had parked the car, where Mum was supposed to have slammed the car door and spoken aggressively to him before he hit her with a hammer twice on the head. It seemed impossible that it would not have reacted to so much noise and disturbance. It was beginning to seem to me that there was no way Sutcliffe had driven his car into the car park as he had claimed. But I hadn't got a clue what to make of this discovery. I felt very disturbed and uncomfortable. Pictures that I had been carrying in my mind for almost thirty years were beginning to look as if they might be fabrications. But what new images should I use to replace them?

I wondered if Sutcliffe might have followed Mum into the field as she headed up the path towards our house, and then attacked her. But that still didn't explain why the dog hadn't barked. I wondered how much noise is made when someone is hit over the head with a hammer.

I thanked John for his time and left him a copy of my book. I didn't explain the 'copy-cat theory' to him. He was elderly and I didn't want to give him something to worry about. I left and drove home in the snow, trying to make sense of what I'd just discovered.

The media did attend the press conference in small numbers and the local news station ran a story, although the main theme was not about the 'copy-cat theory' but of how a member of one victim's family (me) was angered by the allegations. Another journalist from a tabloid newspaper who I spoke to told me they were fed up of hearing about O'Gara and his theory.

One of the services Samaritans carry out is to visit Armley prison in Leeds on a weekly basis. Armley also happens to be the institution where I served my sentence in 1997. Inside there are prisoners who act as 'listeners'. Their role is to listen to any inmates who are going through a hard time. Often this means first-time prisoners who are finding it difficult to come to terms with their loss of freedom, although there could be many reasons a prisoner might be distressed. I'd felt that way when my girlfriend at the time, Jenny, had ended our relationship while I was in Armley. Samaritan visitors acted as a support network for these listeners, as well as dealing with any prisoners who might not have managed to see a listener.

I decided I would put myself forward as a potential visitor. The first step was to go back into the prison for the next volunteers' open day. I mentioned to Ben, the prison coordinator, that I'd been in prison myself and he told me he didn't see that as a problem.

Around a dozen of us met at the new visitors' entrance, which had been built since I had left. It felt strange to be going back voluntarily into the place that had held me against my will for six months. We had to hand in our ID. I produced my passport and half expected my details to be checked and the guard behind the glass window to ask me to step to one side.

We moved through a secure glass waiting area leading to another open area. We were now in the prison and I had to pinch myself. Prison guards were walking around us, checking in for work and chatting normally. While we were waiting in this area to be given our passes I recognised one of the guards. He had been on the prison hospital wing where I had been housed and had worked as a cleaner. I was nervous about starting a conversation with him, mainly because I wasn't sure what he would make of me being there. As he walked past me, I nodded and gave him a small smile, hoping he would remember me. I wanted him to know how I'd turned my life around since I last saw him. He did smile back but automatically; he didn't seem to know who I was.

Being back there brought it home to me how much I had achieved in the seven years since 1997. When I walked out of Armley prison back then my life had crashed down around me and I had considered ending it all. I could never have envisaged being in the situation I was in right now and I thought I might be able to help others to turn their lives around in the same way.

Once we had our passes we were taken through the prison, firstly, funnily enough, to the hospital wing. Of course, I knew full well how it was run. We were taken from the hospital to other parts of the prison, introduced to guards and listeners, and shown round the newly built reception area, where prisoners would stay for the first few days until they came to terms with the fact that they were in prison. It was a lot more inviting than the wing I was placed in when I first arrived.

We were then taken to the chaplain where another listener chatted to us for a while. It certainly felt as though the prison had become more aware of the emotional needs of prisoners. Suicides at Armley still happened, they told us, albeit less frequently, but drugs were still a major problem.

After the visit we were given an application form to fill in so that we could be checked for security. On the form we had to declare if we had any previous convictions. There was no point withholding my drugs conviction, as they would find out anyway. I hoped they would understand where I was in my life and that I was now on the straight and narrow.

A few weeks later the news came that, due to what was on my application form, I'd been turned down as a volunteer. I was a little disappointed but I could understand their decision. I had been a convicted drug dealer in the past and with the serious problem of drugs in prison I could see how they might view me as a risk. The press could have had a field day if they'd ever found out. But it seemed a shame that someone who actually knew what it was like to be in prison, but who also knew how to recover his life afterwards, should not be able to contribute.

On 15 December 2004 the *Sun* announced that Sutcliffe was engaged to be married. I read the coverage with a feeling of mounting horror. The woman, they said, was now wearing his engagement ring. To me it seemed like just another reason to splash the face that had haunted us all our lives across the front pages once more, dragging up all the feelings I had hoped I was leaving behind. The reporter described how the woman in question was 'made up', meaning, I guess, that she was happy. I felt nothing but anger. Why would any woman want to marry a man who had murdered so many other women? The paper went on to report how Sutcliffe thought he would one day be released.

Weddings were happy things, about love and commitment. It seemed unfair that this madman would ever be allowed to feel such joy. Surely he forfeited that right when he took the lives of his victims and ruined the lives of those who survived? Whatever I did, I thought, my past still dogged me. The climb towards happiness seemed to get steeper, just when I had thought it was getting easier. Sometimes it felt that for every step I took forward, I took two back.

But at least I now had Helen, someone I could be sure of, just as long as she wasn't put off by my past.

chapter twelve

Things Can Change

I needn't have worried. The more Helen discovered about me, the more she accepted me. When she finally read the book she put my prison experience down as a 'silly mistake'. I could tell she was going to be behind me all the way with everything I was hoping to achieve in life. It was a huge weight off my mind.

'You're absolutely doing the right thing,' she assured me, 'using any proceeds from the book to get an education.'

One thing I was also becoming aware of was that if our relationship blossomed and we went on to have a family, Helen would be a great wife and mother. Whenever I found myself thinking thoughts like that I had to rein myself in, aware I was being a little premature with my plans. I guess most unmarried people in their mid-thirties are thinking about more than just whether or not they get on over a drink when they meet someone new.

Things weren't perfect between us, and I would be foolish to think there weren't still some minor insecurities on my part, but I was definitely feeling much more confident than I had in past relationships, when even the smallest thing would set me off, making me impossible to live with. Despite this improvement, however, I still struggled at the beginning of the relationship with the fact that another man was interested in Helen. This guy wouldn't take no for an answer, which made me deeply uneasy.

He kept on phoning. Even after Helen had told him she'd met me and wasn't interested he would call every so often to see if we had split up. It took me a couple of months before I trusted Helen completely. It wasn't that she'd done anything to give me reason to suspect her; I just couldn't shake off my old fears of losing someone I cared about. I knew what we both had was special and the problem was with me not her, so I had to take a leap of faith and force myself to ignore this man if I didn't want to risk ruining the best thing that had happened to me in a long time. After a few months my faith was repaid and he stopped calling.

Helen was so caring, not just towards me, but towards everyone she knew or came across in her work. She was so considerate of my feelings, so reliable, trustworthy and honest. She was always there to comfort me whenever I was faced with something difficult, willing to give up any amount of her time to make me feel better.

In the past, with previous relationships, if I had a disagreement or argument with my girlfriend, I would worry I'd shown a side that was like Dad. I'd become angry and defensive, blaming everyone else except myself, and looking for a fight. The worry would sometimes eat away at me, causing me to become even angrier, increasing the chances that I would behave like him. But I knew I must have come a long way over the last few years because this fear was not affecting my relationship with Helen. We could have arguments like anyone else and would quickly make up. This sense of security within the relationship was something I'd always wanted. It was as though there was an awareness between us that this relationship was different to all the others. Helen was definitely special. Although she lived in Sheffield I had no problems driving the thirty-five miles once or twice a week to see her. She had also started staying with me in Leeds, too.

Although I felt I was falling in love, I didn't want to appear needy. So I was pleased when Helen announced one night that she wanted to tell me something. She told me how much she felt about me and that she wished there was a word between 'like' and 'love', as love sounded too strong after knowing someone for so short a time.

'I feel the same,' I assured her.

This was when I really started to fall in love with her, knowing it wasn't one-sided. It was as though another weight was being lifted off my shoulders and our love grew stronger and stronger as the months passed.

'Have you got any of your mum's belongings?' Helen asked one day.

'No,' I admitted. 'None.'

'I think you should contact the police,' she suggested, 'to see whether there's anything held in the files.'

I wondered why I'd never thought of it before. I rang Iona, Mum's youngest sister, and told her what I was thinking of doing.

'That's funny,' she said, 'because I contacted the police recently to ask about a letter your mum sent me just before she was killed. The police asked to borrow it to see if there were any clues in it as to who might have killed her, like an ex-boyfriend or something. That letter would give us a little insight into her personality; how she felt and thought, her writing style and so on. I thought it would be nice to have it back.'

Now that I knew it existed, I hoped the letter would turn up and asked Iona the name and number of the officer who was looking into it for her. I then rang him and explained who I was and that I wanted to know if they had any of Mum's belongings. I wondered, for instance, if they might still have her handbag. I'd heard that when she was found, the handle of the bag was wrapped around her wrist, as if she was protecting it from being stolen.

'I'm going to be looking for the letter for Iona,' the officer told me, 'so I'll look for any belongings while I'm there. I'll call you as soon as I can.'

That was the best I could hope for. It had, after all, been almost thirty years.

At Grandma Newlands' funeral I'd met one of Mum's brothers, Norman, and discovered he lived only fifty miles away from Leeds in the coastal town of Hull. I'd called him a couple of times since and arranged to go over and meet him and his family. Helen couldn't come with me as she was working all weekend, as she often did.

I drove to Hull and was warmly welcomed at the door by Norman and his wife of thirty years, Jackie. As I went into the living room I could hear children and other voices. Norman's two children, Tyrone and Corena, were there with their children; more cousins I never even knew existed. Corena was very slightly built and reminded me of Mum in some way. I'd been told that Mum had been very slim.

After an hour or so of catching up on the missing years, exchanging photos and being told memories of Mum, Norman offered to drive me to the house of one of his brothers. Isaac was the one uncle we were in contact with for the first few years after Mum died. He'd been married to Vicky back then and we would often spend the weekend at their house. As we drove over to Isaac's house, Norman, who had his own building business, told me of his plans for the future. It was nice to hear how successful he was in comparison to my father, who could have done the same but chose only to work as and when he needed some cash. Often on a Monday morning whoever was giving Dad a lift to work would be knocking at the door and Dad would send one of us down to tell them he wasn't going in. He was frequently too hungover and I found it embarrassing even back then.

We arrived at Isaac's house. Although we'd seen one another at the funeral the previous year we didn't really chat then as Isaac was understandably upset at his mother's death. This time we were able to talk more easily. He was in his work clothes, having come straight from a building site. Mum's brothers were all grafters and had worked with their hands all their lives. It was this desire for work that initially brought them from Inverness, where the family had settled, to Leeds in search of jobs. It was because Mum had followed her brothers that she had ended up in Leeds and met Dad.

After a couple of hours we headed back over to Norman's house to eat and get ready to go out to their local social club.

At the end of a great night I sat and spoke with Norman alone about his memories of Mum, and the next day I spent a few more hours with them before driving back to Leeds, promising I would bring Sonia over to see them as soon as I could. I felt that I was getting somewhere in building up a picture of Mum that was about more than just the last few hours of her life.

I was still worrying about the 'copy-cat theory' and had been trying to get hold of any books on Sutcliffe's crimes that I might not have read in the past, to see if I might stumble across anything that might corroborate it. One of the books I bought was called *Voices from an Evil God* by Barbara Jones in which the author writes:

He realises that the families of the women he killed must hate him for what he did, and resent the fact that he is leading a safe and secure life now, at the taxpayers' expense. 'I thought about writing to them [he said], trying to explain about myself. Why I did what I did, and why they ought to try and understand me. I'd like them to know I'm not a monster.'

This was the first time I had heard that he had given any thought to us at all. If he truly did feel like that, maybe he had just held back from writing to us because he didn't think we would want to hear from him. I wanted him to know that if he did want to talk, I was very willing to hear what he had to say. I went straight to my computer and started to write Peter Sutcliffe a letter. I quoted the reference from the book and offered to give him the chance of explaining why he took my mother from me. I felt it would also give him the opportunity of informing me if it wasn't him who killed her. Even as I posted the letter, however, I knew it was very unlikely I would hear from him, and that if I did hear, it might not be for weeks. But it was worth a try.

Although the press conference about the 'copy-cat theory', and my conversation with the caretaker, had raised some doubts in my mind with regard to the identity of Mum's killer, I still thought that on balance it was likely to be Sutcliffe. In many of the interviews I'd given to the press after *Just a Boy* was published I was asked what I thought about Peter Sutcliffe. I always replied that I tried not to think about him.

In fact, I had mixed and confused feelings regarding him. On the one hand I knew he'd carried out a series of hideous acts and he had taken my mother from me, but somewhere inside I had a religious belief that told me there was a God and that He would know exactly what I felt and that He would want me to forgive Sutcliffe. For some people it might sound crazy but that's what I thought. Mum was gone and nothing was going to bring her back. As a result we had the murderer locked behind bars and me outside wanting revenge. It was a stalemate. I wondered if I could take the brave decision to forgive him, would that bring something positive into the situation? I had given a lot of thought to the idea of forgiveness over the years, but had not yet been able to imagine myself doing it.

Would I be letting Mum down by forgiving Sutcliffe? Or would she be proud to see her son forgiving her killer? Something inside me tried still to make sense of what Sutcliffe had done, to find a logical reason for his behaviour. Maybe something terrible had happened in his childhood. I just couldn't accept that my mother's life could be taken so brutally for no justifiable reason. There had to be some kind of explanation. I wondered if this was the only way I could accept her death, by discovering it was the result of a chain reaction of events unknown to me.

Sometimes I found it difficult to accept I was in the position I was; my own life story seemed like something that must have happened to someone else. When people are being warned about the potential dangers of something they want to do, they often say, 'That won't happen to me' or 'These things happen to other people.' I suppose you have to think like that or you would never have the courage to leave the house at all. But bad things do happen, and the people they happen to are normal people, who are living their lives and confidently planning for a future when the rug is suddenly pulled from under their feet and they're shown just how fragile life is.

At the London SAMM meeting one of the expert speakers, a chartered clinical psychologist called David Trickey, had given a presentation about trauma and how it affected children who had suffered a murder in the family. I was intrigued by what he had to say and got hold of some notes from one of his previous speeches.

He talked about bereavement being the 'loss of our assumptive world', meaning that the life we had assumed we would lead, had perhaps even taken for granted, had suddenly been taken away. He also pointed out that every person will react in different ways to trauma. There are, however, certain patterns. Someone who has suffered bereavement in childhood, for instance, is five times more likely to have psychological and psychiatric problems later in life. This did not surprise me. Such a person is also twice as likely to suffer from depression in adulthood and is more likely to attempt suicide.

There were certain things, he said, which could help a child find a straight path through this emotional minefield. When I read the list it made me laugh out loud – nothing that should have happened had ever happened to us.

For example, bereaved children need to say goodbye in some way, which we were never permitted to do. We did not go to Mum's funeral or stand at the graveside. Then they need practical help, which my father was completely incapable of giving, and social support, which was never allowed through the door. Dad had often dismissed people offering help as 'do-gooders'.

My opinion of the social services is a mixed one. I do believe they let us down by allowing us to be placed with such a violent father. It was obvious they hadn't carried out an assessment on him or they would have discovered he was ill equipped to bring up four ordinary children, let alone four traumatised ones. On one occasion, I'm told, Aunty Vicky and Uncle Isaac phoned the social services, as they were concerned about what was going on at home, particularly with Angela, 'the black sheep of the family' as Dad used to describe her; Vicky had noticed a hand mark across her face one weekend. The social services did come but we were spoken to at home, in front of Dad. He just couldn't understand that he didn't have the right to control us. We were his children and it had nothing to do with anyone else. Vicky told me recently that the next time she came to collect us, Dad had slammed the door in her face.

What we actually needed was someone to let us know that what was going on at home shouldn't be allowed, a caring nurse or social worker, for example. We didn't get that. When Sonia was taken from home by the NSPCC, after Dad had given her one of his most brutal beatings, we were not interviewed. No close eye was kept on the rest of us. On reflection, this was unforgivable. After all, it was the 1980s not the 1960s.

Being a child should be all about making mistakes and pushing boundaries. Dad should have been there to keep us in check, to show us right from wrong, but he did it in such a way that he created enormous damage, which has taken me years to correct. I wonder whether my sisters will ever recover. Social services had a duty of care to ensure we were placed with a suitable parent or guardian. It was obvious, looking back, that they had failed to protect us all and it caused years of misery for each of us.

They still make the same mistakes today. In the 1980s they were accused of taking children away from families without just cause and in recent years it appears there has been a reversal in policy. Nowadays social workers seem to try and keep families together, but I fear this tactic leads to many children remaining in families that cause them damage, creating yet more dysfunctional adults and more generations of suffering.

Bereaved children should be encouraged to talk about their loss and their feelings, in order to stand a better chance of making sense of death. They need to be able to express their grief and work through the pain, and their self-esteem needs to be carefully nurtured. Self-esteem has been a problem for most of my life, but even more so when I was a young child. I always hated what I saw in the mirror.

If only we had been able to talk about Mum as often as we thought about her. I couldn't make sense of death as a young child and if only someone had sat me down and talked to me, to get me to open up and explain how I was thinking, maybe then things would not have gone as badly as they did. Even with that sort of help, however, we would still have had the problem of a brutal father who was likely to erupt every time he had a drink. I always felt as though death was just around the corner for me, too, as if some imaginary force or being was gunning against me, determined to take my life. At a more tangible level I also feared that Mum's killer was out there looking for me.

Sometimes I imagine a young child, maybe my own child, experiencing these thoughts and feelings and it breaks my heart. But when I think of it happening to me I don't seem to be able to acknowledge what I went through, what Mum went through. It would have been different had Dad been the one murdered. He was a stranger to me back then. I would have felt little in the way of loss. Whatever attachment I might have had to him had disappeared soon after he left Mum to fend for herself with four young children. As an adult, however, I have to remember that Dad was probably a product of his own upbringing. When I was a boy Dad had told me how his Father had beaten him.

The memory of walking to the bus stop a week before my sixth birthday to look for my mother doesn't feel such a big deal to me. It happened, we waited, we returned, Mum wasn't home. I think of it matter-of-factly. But if I think of another child, a niece or nephew of mine, in the same position I find it almost unbearable to imagine. One of the ways in which we survive trauma, I learned from Caroline, is to 'split off' the bad experience as though it has not happened to us, so that we don't have to bear the pain. Through therapy, gradually the pain is faced in a safe place.

Even today I'm not sure whether or not I have grieved for Mum. My children will never get to meet their grandmother, I will never be able to visit her on Mothers' Day, Christmas and birthdays, or when I'm feeling low and just want to be with her. It's at those moments I realise what has happened and I feel the true extent of my sadness. But I quickly push it away and carry on with whatever I was doing before.

Children bereaved of a significant attachment figure, in traumatic circumstances, often suffer enormous subsequent disruptions such as remaining family members feuding, adults reluctant to talk about it, professionals reluctant to help. Support from families, friends, volunteers and professionals can't make it right, but it can often help.

Sonia and I were placed with two different foster carers. The first didn't show any compassion at all and made us stand and wash the sheets when we'd wet the bed, ensuring that we felt ashamed. The second did make us feel warm, secure and cared for. There were many offers to foster us at the time, including, as I have since discovered, our own family on Mum's side, but Dad wanted us and he had first call.

The authorities let us down by not carrying out a full assessment of Dad. If they had interviewed family members they would have discovered he was a violent man. But then again, maybe he would have been able to fool them. At times he was fine, and in those early months it did seem that things were going to be OK, but it didn't last.

There is something very tangible that the authorities can do to help children in our situation. If we'd been shown a video at school explaining that beatings were something we didn't have to suffer, then perhaps one of us would have turned to a teacher and explained what was going on at home. But at the time I believed Dad was a force to be reckoned with, all-powerful and invincible. He could do whatever he wished because he was our father. I didn't understand that he had no right at all to behave as he did.

Spokespeople for the social services are always saying that things are getting better, that children in families like ours wouldn't fall through the net any more, that someone would be checking on us. I'm sure many thousands of children are looked after well by people working hard on their behalf. But still children are found neglected, beaten or dead. A recent case in Sheffield, where five children under eight were found severely neglected, only came to light because the parents thought one of the children was dead and an ambulance was called. The children were malnourished and one of them was found to have maggots in her nappy. The parents, on the other hand, had everything they wanted in the way of electrical goods and Playstations while the children went without food. Things can change, but before that happens we have to accept that they need to.

* * *

One of the good things about writing *Just a Boy* was that it prompted a lot of people from my past to make contact. I received an email from an old school friend through Friends Reunited, telling me she remembered how I'd stood up in class and read out an essay entitled 'My Family'. I'd assumed that by the 1980s, and after moving from the middle school I'd attended when Sutcliffe was on the loose, most of the kids in high school hadn't known about our past, but her email made me think I must have always wanted to tell the world about what we had been through:

… In my vague recollection, after you had recited your essay, I remember thinking that the teacher should perhaps not have selected this specific topic but that he perhaps was not aware of your past. Incidentally, you chose to read aloud, you weren't selected. Your content was not specific to your ordeal or your mother's ordeal as such, however, for people aware of your situation, it was more than apparent when reading between the lines. I believe it was more about your life without your mother. I remember you mentioning you and Sonia as small children and I am sure you touched on your dad's behaviour as I remember being shocked.

I was aware that your sisters were a little off the rails

but you were the complete antithesis of them from what I recollect throughout the years I knew you. Whatever the content, I remember the room falling into an abyss of absolute silence for only a few seconds but what seemed like an eternity. I remember catching Deborah Lambert's eye who was sitting near me. Looking back I feel it was like you were saying, OK, I have said it now it's out in the open, let's get on with it.

To have got up there and told the class what was going on at home must have been a cry for help. Looking back I wondered why the teacher hadn't informed the authorities about what I'd said. Maybe he was yet to learn the skill of reading between the lines. I hoped that I would never miss something so obvious.

As I got to know my mentor, Eileen, and cousin Caroline, the child psychotherapist, we discussed what I'd written about in *Just a Boy* in more detail. They suggested there was a lack of feelings in the book. I had to admit I still wasn't sure how I felt about everything. This, I was beginning to understand now, was a protective mechanism and it would probably take a lifetime's work to get to where I wanted to be.

———

I still missed Mum immensely, that was obvious, but my anger for Sutcliffe was, for the most part, hidden away. I knew I had a right to feel rage for what he'd done, to want revenge, to want him dead, but part of me didn't want to feel those things as I went about my daily life. I feared that if I allowed myself to hate I would be at risk of becoming like Dad. But I was starting to think that this might not be the best course of action. Why shouldn't I feel hatred towards the man who murdered my mother?

As a young boy I'd thought about revenge, not specifically on Mum's killer, who had at the time yet to be caught, but on society in general. I felt as if the world around me had a life of its own and it had taken Mum from me. My imagined revenge back then was of roaming the streets in a similar fashion to Sutcliffe, killing random males. So, although there may have been a perceived lack of feelings in my book, I knew there had been evidence of strong and abnormal ones along the way. This apparent lack of feelings may also have been as a result of not having developed the capacity to express them. I certainly hadn't seen this in my father whose only strong feelings seemed to be ones of anger.

I have learned from meeting and talking to people through SAMM that nothing is normal after an event like murder. Normality disappears from the lives of those affected, even though it still surrounds them as other people get on with their daily business. What they go through is something that no one can ever be prepared for, so there are no rules on how to behave.

Many people over the years, including my father, have said I must 'move on' and 'put it behind me', but people who have been bereaved in tragic circumstances can never live life in the same way again. Now that I was feeling more secure with myself and my relationship, however, I was moving on but in a different way, able to acknowledge and respect my feelings, even if they included anger and rage. I felt as though they were less likely to be damaging if they were met head on.

Caroline and I talked about how I was able to survive what was going on around me and within me. One possibility was that I'd inherited a strong survival instinct from my mother's family. My maternal grandparents had always had to travel, with their eleven children, to wherever they could find work, just to keep food on the table. Equally Mum had come to Leeds to make a better life for herself and she'd had to fight for it, often literally, where Dad and her boyfriends were concerned. Possibly a similar instinct for survival had helped me and my sisters keep ourselves together through those dark times. When we received beatings from Dad, each of us knew it would be over eventually and that we would survive. I spent my time wishing those years away, looking forward to the day that I would be old enough to leave the house. Two of my sisters left at the age of fourteen, so it must have been the same for them. Not that it did them any good. They're both still struggling all these years later, and Dad still fails to see how his behaviour influenced us all.

'It's like you're being held together with thin threads,' Caroline said, which was a good interpretation of how I'd felt. At times in the past just getting through the day was a task – interacting with people, fighting the feeling that I was not liked or that people could see my history and would think badly of me. How stupid that felt now. How could anyone feel as though we were at fault for anything that went on in our childhoods?

The first five years of our lives are said to be the most formative and although there were instances of violence around the house, most of my memories of that time were happy ones. Yes, poverty and unemployment were rife on the estate, but life for me then was good, or so part of me wanted to remember. In fact, life was probably pretty dreadful and Mum's certainly wasn't perfect, but even with all her shortcomings, she was 'good enough' to get us through and she loved us unconditionally. I figured it was those early years of love that kept me from going completely off the rails later.

For most of my adult life I have had a desire to meet someone with whom I could re-experience some of the love I had had before Mum died. With Helen I finally felt as if I had a chance.

I know now that it's essential for many like me to receive therapy to survive trauma, but I've heard from so many people since the book's publication about how they just couldn't get the help they needed. If it was offered at all it was nearly always too little and too late. I heard from people who'd had to travel to America in order to get the therapy and support they needed. Why was it we couldn't get what we needed in Britain?

At the SAMM meeting in London I asked Michaela what sort of help she'd received after her father had been killed. She told me that when she contacted her doctor she was told she'd have to wait six weeks to be seen. Stories like this always annoy me. After big disasters special counselling crisis centres are set up to deal with the masses of people who have been affected, but often the facilities are not available to individuals like us. So much money is spent on rehabilitating offenders – and I imagine that millions have been spent on Sutcliffe – but nothing was given to help me or my sisters deal with traumatic emotions that were caused by him carrying out his first murder.

chapter thirteen

Family Life

Helen invited me to spend Christmas with one of the families she'd nannied for in London and whom she now regarded as part of her own extended family. I was happy to drive down with her.

The parents obviously took family life seriously. They loved their kids and it was nice to know they appreciated Helen so much that they included her in their plans each Christmas. It seemed to be more evidence that she truly was something special. All the children she had looked after took pleasure in showing me what Helen had created for them. They each had many albums, which read like diaries, filled with treasured memories of all the things Helen had done with them; taking them out for days to interesting, stimulating places, keeping entrance tickets, photos with messages underneath, or the children's own drawings. They were the children's pride and joy.

I couldn't have imagined anything like those albums in my childhood. Parents in the sort of families we came from didn't have the time or inclination for anything like that, not that most of them would have known how to start even if they'd wanted to. Dad's spare time was kept for drinking in the pub. I'd seen programmes over the years explaining why men were attracted to certain women, seeing things in them that would make them good mothers. With Helen I was seeing lots of evidence that she would be a perfect mother and that she would be able to show me how to be a good parent. After all, I had no other role models. The more I got to know her, the more I fell for her. Was it because I'd come across someone who would ensure that my children had the kind of childhood I yearned for? I don't know, but maybe some of that was at work here.

We woke up on Christmas Day and sat in the living room with the family, taking part in what was obviously a traditional family ritual. Everyone there, including the adults, opened a present one at a time in turn as we sat in a circle. For everyone else there it was normal, but for me it was something completely new and wonderful.

I knew that when I had children in the future I would certainly adopt the traditions of this family. Maggie, the children's mother, organised a treasure hunt, something else that I believe had been passed down through her family. There were four teams of three who set off round the high street trying to answer questions such as 'how many clowns are in town?', the answer being found on a poster on a wall somewhere. I tried to imagine my father ever going to so much trouble and using so much imagination to entertain and educate his children.

The adults then did the *Guardian* quiz of the year's news stories, followed by a walk with the whole family on the nearby common.

While we were down in London we visited another family who Helen had nannied for in the 1980s. They lived in Chelsea and the children were now aged twenty-two and nineteen. For the first time they were able to cook a meal for their ex-nanny. Helen confided that it felt strange, having them in the kitchen cooking for us. It was obvious to me how highly they thought of her and how much they loved her. It seemed that these families looked on their children as beings to nurture and encourage, rather than control and punish.

After dinner we watched old videos of the family in Hong Kong, on a film set. Their father was a film producer and had taken Helen and the children wherever he travelled to. It was so nice to be around families who were so different to the one in which I was brought up. I doubted that either set of parents would even be able to imagine taking a stick to their children, forcing them under the water in the bath or drowning their pet dog.

The more I got to see how others lived, the more I reckoned that Dad was a poor excuse for a father. I knew that if I did have children, I wouldn't want him to see them, although I didn't even know whether he would want to see them anyway. I heard he'd bragged to people in the pub that he was a granddad again but failed to tell them he hadn't actually been to see the child and had only come across him at his christening.

We spent four days in London and arranged to meet up with Judy, the literary agent who had represented me for *Just a Boy*. On the last night Helen and I went out for a romantic meal and spent some time alone, before driving back to Leeds the next day. It had been an eye-opening trip for me. I had seen the sort of life I wanted, and I knew who I wanted to spend it with.

After Christmas I renewed my search for the children of Peter Sutcliffe's other victims. Having taken as much information as I could out of the books I had read, I went back to the library in Leeds and started to look through the old newspaper cuttings, which were stored on reels of microfiche.

Sutcliffe's second victim was 42-year-old Emily Jackson,

who was married to Sydney and had three children. She was found on 21 January 1976, the day my mother was buried. As I came to the cutting for 20 January, the night Emily was killed, I pictured people reading the *Yorkshire Evening Post* on the way home from work that night, or in the comfort of their sitting rooms, and I imagined what Emily Jackson might have been doing that evening, unaware that it was her last. Maybe she was reading the same words that were in front of me now, probably at the same time as she made an evening meal for the family, the same way Mum did for us the night before she died.

I was aware of my own breathing in the quiet room as I slowly turned the handle which brought the next day's head-lines into view, pausing as if I might actually have the power to influence the course of events by not bringing them up on the projector in front of me. I turned the reel until eventually the headline was there for me to see, above a picture of Emily's children.

I went through Sutcliffe's five-year campaign of terror in the same way, taking notes from the newspapers of any names, ages and addresses I could find, until I had all the identities of the other children in full. Excluding me and my sisters, there were nineteen. I'd been thinking about these children for over twenty-five years, and I felt as though I was finally on my journey to find them. I wasn't sure whether I would be successful, but I knew that now was the time to try. Filming for the documentary was about to start and I had the advantage of the team at the production company to help me.

Once I had the details I started sifting through the electoral roll. I soon realised just what a massive task I was facing. The first person I looked for was Emily Jackson's son, Christopher. There were thirteen possible Christopher Jacksons in Leeds. I set about composing a letter to send to each one, and hoped no one would find it offensive.

In the end I sent out around two hundred letters and then sat back to wait. I realised there was a strong possibility all the people I was seeking would have moved out of the area, wanting to get as far away as possible from the scene of their childhood unhappiness. There was a risk that none of the names I'd written to were the right ones. Each morning I almost ran to check the mail, but nothing arrived.

One morning, however, an envelope arrived that was stamped with the postmark of the town where Broadmoor was located. I knew it had to be a reply to the letter I had sent to Sutcliffe at the secure hospital where he was incarcerated. I opened it tentatively, my heart thumping in my ears, wondering whether he had actually written the letter himself. Was I finally going to be communicating with him directly after all these years?

The letter looked official. It was from the prison doctor. I read slowly, wanting to take it all in properly.

The doctor confirmed he'd received my letter and promised he would be discussing its contents with his patient shortly and that he would write to me again as soon as he could. I was amazed. Sutcliffe was actually going to be forced to talk about me? I tried to imagine how he would feel to hear from me and what kind of reply I would get. The more I thought about it the more I felt the most likely outcome would be some attempt to manipulate me. Was this such a good idea? I wondered.

All I could do was wait.

chapter fourteen

Stepping Back into the Past

After so many years of searching for pictures of Mum, so we could have a more realistic image of her than the one they always used in the press, Iona, Mum's sister, found a passport photograph at the bottom of a trunk in her house. She rang to tell me.

'It's the clearest picture of her I've ever seen,' she said.

I couldn't wait to see my copy, which arrived in the post the next day. When I opened the envelope and took out the small black and white photo I almost cried. It looked just like me, except Mum had a full head of dark hair. I was her double. I stared and stared at her, wishing her to come alive.

In October it would be thirty years since Mum died. Iona and I agreed we should arrange an anniversary at her graveside in Leeds, and a memorial service. It seemed fitting that we should say a formal goodbye, which we'd never really done.

I went to visit Alex, a photographer friend, and explained I wanted to blow the photo up to almost life-size and have Mum's name printed at the bottom.

'I can't promise anything,' he said, 'but I'll give it a go.'

As I continued my research into the children of Peter Sutcliffe's other victims, I discovered a Sydney Jackson in the West Yorkshire area telephone book and thought he might be the man who had lost his wife, Emily, back in 1976. I decided to ring from Sonia's house. It was a tense enough situation as it was, but to make it worse the documentary film crew, who were following my progress as I looked for the other children and tried to find out more about Mum and Sutcliffe, had now begun work, and I'd agreed to let them film what was going on.

It took some time to pluck up the courage to dial the number, as I tried in vain to rehearse a few possible opening lines. My breathing was heavy and I was feeling extremely anxious. Sonia was sitting beside me and I could hear the camera filming in the background. Eventually I dialled the number. There was no going back now.

'Hello, can I speak to Sydney, please?'

'Who?' It was a woman's voice. She sounded elderly.

'Sydney Jackson,' I said, continuing after a pause. 'This is Richard McCann.'

'Where from?'

'Son of Wilma McCann.'

'Who?'

This was not going to plan. I expected an elderly man and I was talking to a woman. I had expected that once I mentioned Mum's name they would know who I was immediately. I was finding it difficult to keep it together. I couldn't just put the phone down, however much I might want to. The camera kept turning mercilessly as the words stuck in my throat. The misunderstandings went on for what seemed like an age before I was finally able to ascertain that I had the wrong family. I apologised and hung up.

It had been a nightmare of a call, leaving my emotions in turmoil. My hopes had soared when I thought at first I had the right family, and then they had been dashed. I wrote a letter to the family once I'd calmed down, explaining who I was so they were completely clear, and gave my sincere apologies for disturbing them.

I was beginning to think I was going to need some professional help in this hunt. I had already written a general letter to the children of Sutcliffe's victims and sent it to the police, asking them to pass it on to any of the families they were in touch with, and I had written all those letters to the possible children in the phone book. But nothing had come of it. It seemed that I would have to find another way.

A little over a week later I contacted a private detective, taking every bit of information I could find on all the children of the victims. He worked from a modest office above a shop in a small town near Leeds. He seemed down to earth and told me he normally did find the people he went looking for and that with the list I'd given him he was very hopeful. I left his office after half an hour, full of renewed hope.

Alex, the photographer, rang to say he'd enlarged the picture of Mum. When I went to pick it up I saw he'd also gone to the trouble of having it mounted in a black frame. It was perfect. All the cracks and creases were gone and rather than being black and white it was now sepia, giving the image a slightly golden glow.

The plan was to have it on display somewhere at the anniversary memorial, so everyone would remember Mum as she was and not how the press had portrayed her. All I had to do now was organise the day itself.

* * *

In January Helen went to Cuba with some of her family, including her brother, aunts, uncles and cousins. Originally I was going to go with them but the dates clashed with the start of the university term, as well as with the making of the documentary. The holiday had been booked for a long time so Helen couldn't let everyone down, but I didn't like the idea of being apart from her for sixteen days. From the moment she left it was horrible for us both. We'd started to see a lot of one another by then, fitting in around Helen's work and my university and other commitments, and we missed one another even more than we'd expected.

I phoned her as often as I could, running up almost two hundred pounds on my telephone bill. Helen sent emails every few days and between us we counted the days till we would be back together again. She admitted that missing me so much had spoilt her holiday. I wished I'd made the trip after all.

Helen was due to travel back with the rest of her family from Gatwick early one Friday morning, and because I was working late at Samaritans on Thursday evening we decided I would drive to Sheffield station and be waiting for her train.

As soon as my shift was over I drove home and tried to get to sleep as fast as possible so that our reunion would arrive more quickly. But try as I might, I just couldn't get myself to sleep so at 12.30 a.m. I got out of bed and went to make myself a drink. I was simply too excited about seeing her again to be able to settle. I decided not to meet her at Sheffield station. I'd missed Helen's birthday while she was away so I packed up her presents and made the long drive down the M1 to Gatwick to meet her plane, arriving at 4.45 a.m.

On the way down it was reported on the news that Sutcliffe had been released for the day three days earlier, so he could go to Arnside in Cumbria, where his father's ashes were scattered. Just when I was feeling happier and more excited than I could remember feeling before, his name returned to haunt me. I couldn't understand why the Home Office had decided he should be shown such compassion. He was said to have been too depressed to attend his father's funeral and the doctors thought he needed to visit this place in order to say goodbye.

When Helen appeared through the automatic doors with all her bags, I threw my arms around her. She looked so beautiful after sixteen days in the Cuban sun. I never wanted to be that long apart from her again. She told me on the journey north that she hoped that I would have been there to surprise her but she couldn't believe I had actually done it.

Eventually I told her about the news I'd heard on the way down, but she didn't really want to hear it. I knew she was right. Since we'd met it seemed that every week there was another headline about him. His face was there again and again, reminding us all about Sutcliffe and what he'd done and what he'd taken from us. On the journey home I was getting phone calls from the press asking for comments and Helen was becoming understandably annoyed that it was spoiling the excitement of our reunion.

When we arrived at her home, exhausted, we went to bed and slept throughout the day, not waking till the following morning.

A few days later another news story reported that Sutcliffe had written to the Home Secretary, claiming he should be released from captivity because he'd been locked up for twenty-four years, during which time he'd not committed a crime and was therefore no longer a threat to the public. Twenty-four years of not killing someone when you're in prison hardly guarantees good behaviour once you're back on the outside. It felt that once again Sutcliffe was trying to manipulate the situation to his advantage and I was fearful the authorities would fall for it.

The private detective called to say he believed he had an address for one of the children of Emily Jackson. He'd discovered that the lady in question was the right age, and her marriage details, which can be found on an index available to the public, stated she had the maiden name of Jackson. It also stated her mother's maiden name, which he had discovered was Wood. He said he was 99 per cent sure this was the person we were looking for.

Sonia and I drove to meet him in a café where he gave us the details, warning us to be careful.

'Write to her first,' he advised. 'Let her know who you are.'

We understood what he meant after the embarrassment of our previous attempt, but we were very optimistic. It was great news. The best break so far. We wrote a letter carefully explaining who we were and that we would like to make contact with her. I gave my home address, posted the letter and waited, hoping this time that we would hit the right target.

A few days passed and I received a call from the police officer who was arranging a search through the vaults where all the evidence and files from the investigation were held. I didn't want any smalltalk from him, just confirmation that he'd found something that Mum had worn, owned or held; a bag, a shoe or a watch, or maybe just the letter to Iona.

'There was nothing,' he said, and my heart sank. Later that night my hopes were dashed still further when Iona rang to say she'd received a similar call. No letter had been found. I tried to pretend I wasn't bothered but I was. I'd desperately wanted to have something of Mum's.

Not long after I'd sent the letter to the woman the private detective thought was Emily Jackson's daughter, a neighbour informed me a woman had been sitting outside my house for a few hours. Eventually she'd asked the neighbour some questions about me: Did I work? Was I married? What kind of person was I?

This freaked me out. It was too much of a coincidence. It had to be Emily Jackson's daughter. I assumed she'd received the letter and thought that rather than write to me she would come and find out more about me. I contacted Sonia and we decided the best course of action would be to go and see her. We were sure now we had the correct address.

We drove to the house, which wasn't too far from Sonia's place, and parked round the corner. The documentary cameraman was with us as we sat nervously in the car, building up the courage to knock on the door. We decided I'd do it alone, so as not to overwhelm her. My heart was in my throat as I left the car and approached the nice, neat house. It was nothing like the estates we'd been brought up in. It looked as though she'd done well for herself. As I knocked on the door I started to hope she wouldn't be home, so that I could go back to the safety of the car, but I could see a figure moving at the other side of the window in the front door.

A lady opened the door, looking puzzled at who might be calling on her unexpectedly. She was surrounded by young children. I knew there was no turning back now.

'I'm looking for a Mrs Greene,' I said. 'I believe she lives at this address.'

'I'm not the person you're looking for,' she said. 'But you have got the right address. Mrs Greene moved out a little over a year ago.'

'Did you receive a letter from me, addressed to her?' I asked.

'No,' she said. 'I would have remembered.'

Rather than disappointed, I was actually relieved to have the pressure of the situation lifted, at least temporarily. The tension had almost been too much for me to cope with. The thought of actually being confronted by a person who until then had just been a name in the newspaper was very daunting. I apologised for disturbing her and rushed back to the car to let Sonia know.

We sat for a few minutes and figured out that if the house owner hadn't received our letter, the mail must have been automatically redirected to the new address. What we didn't know was where the new address was. We would have to wait another few days and hope for a letter from her.

Just as we were about to drive off, a young paperboy passed the car and it occurred to me that if anyone could help it would be him. I asked if he knew the family who'd lived in the house. He did remember them but didn't know where they'd moved to. He pointed me to a house close by and told me that this family may know where they'd gone. I knocked there and was told they knew the street name but not the number. Eventually Sonia and I discovered which house it was from their description.

Again we sat in the car for some time, as I tried to build up the courage to knock. Sonia assured me it was OK as it looked as though this woman had come looking for me. By now it was getting late and dark, and finding a stranger on the doorstep was going to be even more alarming. But it was now or never.

As I approached the house, a man and a young child came out. My bottle went and I crossed the road, giving the impression I was heading somewhere else. They got into a car. Once they'd gone I reported back to Sonia, buying myself a bit more time, and then once again headed for the house. At least it looked as if we would be able to talk in privacy. It was possible she had never told her husband about her past and this way he wouldn't have to know I'd called.

It was a large, new, semi-detached house. I knocked at the door, feeling terrible. What if she just wanted to put everything behind her? Then I remembered she'd come looking for me. My mind was churning as fast as my stomach.

A tall, dark-haired woman answered the door, looking puzzled. I had imagined a nice smiling face after she had gone to the trouble of waiting outside my house. I still wasn't completely sure I had the right person.

'My name's Richard McCann,' I said. 'Does that mean anything to you?'

'The Yorkshire Ripper,' she said, taking me by surprise.

'Was your mother Emily Jackson?'

The question seemed to confuse her. She didn't actually reply.

'Where are you getting all this information?' she asked.

'I'm trying to contact the other children who lost their mothers to Sutcliffe. I thought you were the daughter of Emily Jackson. All the information which brought me here was available in the public domain. I haven't done anything underhand in order to find you.'

I didn't want her thinking I'd been going through her rubbish or anything like that.

'I've read your book,' she said, and I could tell by her reaction that she wasn't the woman who'd been sitting outside my house. That must have been someone from the press. There were so many news stories lately; one of the local newspapers must have been wanting to follow up a lead.

'I don't think it's right that you go knocking on strangers' doors like this,' she said.

I didn't have the energy to tell her the chain of events that had led to me making this decision. I could see her point, anyway. I apologised for intruding and headed back to the car. It was a mistake. I shouldn't have done it. She was right; it wasn't appropriate to go knocking on people's doors uninvited. I got in the car, sat back, sighed and told Sonia that it wasn't her.

'Are you sure?' she asked.

'No, I'm not sure, but either way she didn't appreciate me calling on her out of the blue. I feel a bit ashamed.'

We drove home feeling deflated. We thought we'd found someone who wanted to talk to us but we were wrong. It may have been the person we were looking for but one thing was certain – she didn't want to talk to us.

chapter fifteen

More Leads

Despite the setbacks, I was still determined to keep searching. Within a few weeks the private eye had given us six more addresses, one for each of the families in which the victims had children at the time of their deaths. Sonia and I figured that if we could find one child from each family then they would pass us on to the others if they were interested in making contact. We still felt optimistic, eagerly sending out the letters before settling back once again to wait.

A week or so passed and our spirits began to sink once more. Just as we were resigning ourselves to the idea that we were not going to get any response at all, Sonia received a call on her mobile from a lady whose mother was another of Sutcliffe's victims. Sonia was over the moon, her optimism restored in a swoop.

'She chatted for ages,' she told me. 'She'd just been out shopping and she called me from the bus on her way home. She said she wanted to get to know me and asked me to send her a letter.'

We both decided to write to her to tell her more about our lives and how we felt. In my letter I explained how we'd always wondered about how the other children were getting on and told her I was offering the hand of friendship to her. I explained how helpful I'd found speaking to the other members of SAMM, and assured her we were here for her and her family.

Neither of us ever heard from her again.

It was a huge disappointment. Once again we were feeling down and with no replies from anyone else I wondered just how all these people were handling life. Had they all decided the best policy was to bury the past? Were they right?

I wondered if we would have felt the same had we had a chance to grieve properly and to remember our mother as we grew up. Maybe our desire to search for these people was driven by our need to find out more about Mum and our past, whereas the others were perhaps comfortable with what they knew and didn't want to open old wounds unnecessarily.

A number of the children of Sutcliffe's other victims had either been adopted before their mothers were killed or were adopted due to the deaths. It was possible these people might know nothing about their pasts. Irene Richardson, for instance, had had two children who she put up for adoption when she was having a hard time. She had then gone on to have two more girls, who were still living with their mother when she was killed and were also adopted soon after. I didn't attempt to contact any of them in case they knew nothing about their birth mother at all.

Then, completely out of the blue, I received an email from Alan, the only son of Irene Richardson. He'd received my email address from Noel O'Gara, the man who had developed the 'copy-cat theory'. I was delighted to hear from him. In his letter he described how he'd known he was adopted since he was a teenager but had chosen never to do anything about it. His adoptive parents had given him a very happy childhood and he had never felt short of love. The previous year, however, he'd decided he wanted to contact his birth mother to show her he'd turned out fine. He had his own business and was married to a lovely woman, with two sons. He wanted his mum to meet her daughter-in-law and two grandchildren, and could even imagine the joy on all their faces at the reunion he would organise.

He'd written to the adoption agency asking for details of his parents and he was given the devastating news that his mother had been killed in 1977 in Leeds. He'd been sent a newspaper article by the adoption agency, which told him the details of his mother's murder. It also carried a picture of her, but did not say who the murderer was or that, some years later, he was caught, tried and found guilty.

Alan also discovered that he had a whole new family who he had yet to meet, especially three sisters who he was now desperate to find. The adoption agency were not able to give Alan any details of who his sisters were or where to find them.

Having discovered he was never going to meet his mother, he left it there for the time being while he tried to absorb the news, thinking that he might one day contact the *Yorkshire Post* to see if they had any more details about who his mother's killer was.

He was doing quite well at putting the revelation to the back of his mind until he heard the news story on the radio about Sutcliffe being released for the day.

He explained that it felt as though everything had fallen into place in his head. Leeds was in Yorkshire and his mother was murdered around the time of the Ripper killings. He realised his mother could have easily been one of Sutcliffe's victims, so he immediately went on to his computer and carried out an Internet search for the Yorkshire Ripper.

One of the first sites he came across was Noel O'Gara's. Alan described how he scrolled through the pictures of all the victims, and there was his mother's face on screen. It was the very same picture he'd seen in the newspaper article that the adoption agency had sent.

As if finding out the previous year that the mother he was searching for had been murdered wasn't enough, now he knew it was by one of the most prolific killers Britain has ever produced. He emailed Noel O'Gara to see if he could help, and perhaps track down his sisters. Noel gave him my details.

I explained that coincidentally I was trying to contact some of the children at the moment and that a documentary about my life was being made for the BBC. The fact that he had only found out about his mother twelve months earlier confirmed we were right not to try and find children who had been put up for adoption. I hoped that any of them who did know the truth of their background would see the documentary and contact me. Maybe if Alan appeared in the film as well, his sisters, or someone who knew them, would see it.

Alan and I exchanged emails for a while, getting to know one another, telling each other what was going on in our lives. Eventually I sent him my phone number and let him know what time I would be at home. I sat nervously waiting for his call at the designated time. He never rang. My heart sank; was this going to turn out to be yet another dead end?

Later he emailed to tell me he found it all a little over-whelming and needed time to think. I assured him I would be there whenever he decided he wanted to talk. I was very excited to have managed to make even this much contact. Here was a man who was the same age as me and both our mothers had died at the age of twenty-eight, at the hands of the same person. That gave us a great deal in common. It also turned out that his mother had travelled south from Scotland, just like mine, in search of a better life. His wife was even called Helen.

As the weeks passed and more stories about Sutcliffe appeared in the news we were able to discuss our feelings about it via emails. Obviously it was more painful for Alan because he was still coming to terms with the whole idea whereas I had been coping with it for as long as I could remember, but the mutual support was helpful for us both. We decided we wouldn't speak on the phone but that we would get together in person instead. We set a date for the following month to meet up in a hotel bar in Leeds. I could hardly wait.

Sixteen days had passed since Sonia had had a drink, the longest she had gone for some years. Helen and I decided to show some support by sending her a bunch of flowers. There wasn't anyone else around to encourage her.

One of the books on the crimes of Sutcliffe I had read was *Deliver Us From Evil*, written by David Yallop in the year before Sutcliffe was arrested when the hunt for the Ripper was the story that consumed the newspapers. In the book David suggested that the man the police were looking for might be a lorry driver in the Bradford area and not a Geordie, as was thought until Sutcliffe was arrested. David seemed to be able to see things the police couldn't, and I thought he might be able to help throw some light on O'Gara's 'copy-cat theory'. I also wanted to ask him if he knew any more about Mum, particularly about the accusation that she had been a prostitute, which had always worried me and continued to do so.

I was able to make contact and asked if I could visit him. He lived near London and I drove down to meet him at his home, with the film crew in tow. I was extremely nervous but he soon put me at my ease, inviting me into his large, detached house, set in enormous grounds. I started by asking what he thought about the 'copy-cat theory', once we were as comfortable as it was possible to be with the cameras on us.

'I know you've been unsettled by what the man over the

water has been saying,' he said, referring to O'Gara. He went on to say he thought the theory was little more than a fairytale and that I shouldn't give it any more of my time.

'O'Gara is saying Sutcliffe is blood group "O" not "B". It's nonsense,' he said. 'I made some mistakes in the book because it was written before Sutcliffe was arrested, but I didn't get the blood group wrong. I checked that not only with the police but, while he was waiting in Wakefield prison, I checked it with the medical people there, so there is no doubt whatsoever that his blood group is "B". O'Gara is saying Sutcliffe accepted wrongly that he had murdered thirteen women and attempted to murder a further seven, offering the defence that he didn't do it but that he was schizophrenic, "voices from God" and all that.

'So first of all you have to have the principal man admitting to a huge number of crimes he didn't commit, you then have to have the police – who had a full statement from him, it took eighteen hours to get it all down, I think, over a period of days – the police being part of a conspiracy, not only senior ranks but also junior ranks, the ones actually taking the statements. And then you have all the doctors who would have to know, as they would be examining Sutcliffe. Then the Crown Prosecution would have to know, probably up to the level of Home Secretary. So what we're talking about here is a suggestion that something like two hundred people in our country at varying degrees of authority actually sat down and conspired. Why would they do this? Why would Sutcliffe allow them to do this?'

When he put it like that it did seem pretty unlikely.

'I have no doubt,' he said, 'that your mother was murdered by Sutcliffe.'

We talked for a while about the details of the Ripper murders, and then I asked the question that had been on my mind for so long.

'I think, even in your book, it's reported that twenty-nine of Mum's boyfriends were questioned. Do we know whether or not they were clients of hers?'

'That's not in my book,' he replied. 'Your mother was a woman who enjoyed life to the full. You'll know more about her marriage than me but I don't think it was a happy one. In fact at the time of her death—'

'They were separated, yes,' I interrupted, to reassure him that I knew.

'Your mum would go out for a night's fun. Now I had a mum, God rest her soul, so I can empathise very much with Wilma. My mum would go out to the pub and she might come back with a different uncle every so often and I'm sure some of them would be generous and give her money. Now your mother, as far as I knew, had no record for soliciting at all.'

'You see this is the puzzling thing,' I said. 'If Mum had no record of it and she was only acting in the same way that your mother did, then why would she offer, fifty yards from her home, at one in the morning, to lie on her back for five pounds and have sex with Sutcliffe, as he claimed?'

'I think at the time your mother was drunk and when women are drunk they're susceptible to do things they would-n't do when sober. I think your mother had a drinking problem and was found drunk and disorderly on a few occasions, not soliciting. Now that's a different ball game. I think that alcohol was an important element in Wilma's behaviour pattern. She's not the first person whose behaviour changed when they were drunk, and she won't be the last.

'Your mum was a good person, who had a lust for life like the rest of us. She wanted to have fun and she was bringing up four children without a stable man around. Now you'd need quite a bit of fun to get through that one. From what I under-stood at the time she was a good mother and undoubtedly loved all of you deeply. That's how you should remember her.

'There's a danger here that if you live in the past too much then you may die in the past. I lost a son some years ago, aged thirty-two. He died suddenly in Melbourne. I didn't even know he was there. I have great trouble coming to terms with that. I can't sit and grieve about that any more than anyone else can when there's a life to be led, when there are things to be done. Closure and the ability to cope with one's grief becomes that much easier when you keep yourself occupied with your own growth.'

I wondered if that was what I'd been doing over the last few years, writing the book, joining Samaritans and going to university.

'That doesn't mean you forget it,' he went on. 'You never forget it. But you begin to get proportion and perspective with it so it doesn't get to colour every action.'

'It's certainly not doing that,' I assured him. 'I am moving forward.'

'You are. I think you're a very stable young man.'

'It's just this recurring theory that this man O'Gara keeps coming up with.'

'I'm afraid your mother is locked for ever, in my mind, with one of the most notorious serial killers this country has ever seen. But you're talking about your mum, not "Wilma McCann the victim of Peter Sutcliffe". Your mum, Sutcliffe and you are linked in a curious way because of that dreadful night. We have to accept that, and who you choose to tell and who you choose not to tell is up to you.

'The details of these cases eventually fade from the memory unless you have the personal involvement that you have. You'll need to move on and not let it obsess you or preoccupy you. It doesn't mean you lose your mum's memory but that you put it into perspective, so it doesn't dominate and get in the way of your ambitions, what you want to do with your life.'

'I didn't feel this was something I was allowing to take over my life,' I protested. 'It's something I'm learning to come to terms with. It's never going to go away and this "copy-cat theory" has created an element of doubt for me.'

'This is not going to go away and will become like Jack the Ripper. This is why they called Sutcliffe "the Ripper". It sells newspapers and fills television programmes. Someone coming up with an absurd theory about a notorious case will always create interest, and in twenty years' time there will be another theory. I'm as certain as I am about anything in my life about the details of your mother's death and who is responsible for that. The idea of a conspiracy that would involve so many people to wrongfully find a man guilty of thirteen murders when he only did four, not to mention the attempted murders, is absurd. It has no credibility at all.'

Then he gave me some advice.

'You've got a lot of potential and youth, energy and spirit on your side. Don't let this man Sutcliffe spiritually murder you like he physically murdered your mother.'

I became upset at this point, but did all I could to hold back the tears. Noticing I was struggling, David suggested I use the bathroom. I took his advice and left him and the film crew downstairs. Once behind the locked door I burst out crying; it had all been too much for me. All this talk of Mum and trying to put it all into perspective had worn me out emotionally. I sobbed on my own for five minutes before cleaning myself up and returning downstairs.

chapter sixteen

The Search
Continues

A headline in the *Yorkshire Evening Post* announced that 'RIPPER MUST NOT BE FREED', and Sutcliffe's picture was once again on display. The next day I received a telephone call from a Leeds MP, who assured me he would do all he could to get confirmation that Sutcliffe would not be released. Almost a thousand readers wrote in to the paper asking for Sutcliffe to remain behind bars.

The next call came from the *News of the World,* telling me Sutcliffe was planning to write his memoir, in which he would be saying he didn't kill all the women whose murders he had confessed to. No other newspapers ran the story and in the end it was only a few small lines. I decided to take it with a pinch of salt, remembering what David Yallop had said about news-papers loving theories, however ridiculous they might be. It seemed that by standing up and telling my story I had made myself one of the first ports of call for any journalist who had an interest in the Ripper case.

More important was the fact that Sonia got drunk again, after all her hard work.

It had been a few weeks since I received the letter from Sutcliffe's doctor saying he would talk to his patient about answering my questions, so I decided to ring him directly. I left a message and asked him to return my call, which he did a little later as I was driving to Helen's.

He told me he'd read my book and complimented me on it. He explained that Sutcliffe was trying to arrange a visit for me with his legal team and would let me know soon. The news shocked me but I said nothing. My intention had been for him to write to me but it seemed Sutcliffe had misunderstood me and thought that when I asked him to explain his actions to me, I meant in person. That was the last thing on my mind, but now it was almost being offered I simply said I would wait to hear from him. I wanted to work out how I felt before responding.

I put the phone down, unable to believe what I'd just been

discussing. I had been casually talking about meeting the man who had butchered my mother. I wasn't sure that I could trust myself not to attack him if he was sitting right in front of me. Despite these misgivings, I didn't want to rule out the idea of a meeting. I wanted to consider it carefully. Maybe it would be a way forward.

Perhaps, if he met me, Mum would become a reality to him. Maybe then he would see her as a mother who had children and it would bring home what he had done, who he had affected. And by looking me in the eyes and seeing the damage he had caused, he might be forced to feel some remorse.

Over a month had passed since Sonia and I had written to the victims' children and we still hadn't had any replies to the letters. I needed to think of other ways of reaching them while we waited for the documentary to be completed and screened. I contacted the BBC in Leeds to ask if they would allow me to appear on the local news in order to ask the children to make contact, but although I made my appeal on 8 February, that didn't work either.

One of the people who agreed to talk on film about Mum was her old friend Caroline. Sonia went to meet her with the camera crew.

'I never managed to meet a friend quite like her since,' she admitted.

'How did you come to be friends?' Sonia asked.

'Your mum came into this late-night drinking club with your dad,' Caroline explained. 'She walked up to me at the table, leant over and accused me of being interested in her man.'

Fearing for her safety, Caroline had grabbed hold of Mum and started wrestling with her. Mum had come off worse.

They'd bumped into one another again a few days later in Leeds city market, on Butchers' Row.

'I remember she had three of you beside her and another in a pram,' Caroline said. 'I was with my dad and mum. Wilma walked up, stood in front of me and punched me. I was so surprised, she'd walked off before I could say anything.'

The next time they bumped into one another was in another club and once again Mum had walked up to her, this time inviting her to go to the ladies. Not wanting to show fear, Caroline followed her, preparing herself for a fight.

'I want to shake your hand,' Mum told her once they were behind the closed door. 'You're the only woman ever to stand up to me, because I'm the hardest woman in this town.'

I was surprised to hear that she described herself like that, but I felt it gave a little more insight into why Sonia became so aggressive when she'd had a drink. Like Sonia, Mum was the nicest person you could want to meet, when she was sober. She was caring and considerate of other people's feelings. I had never seen Mum aggressive with drink, but I was willing to believe that she had been like that, having seen Sonia in action so many times.

Caroline explained how Mum had told her that we, her children, were all educated in not answering the door if anyone called. I took this to mean we may have been left alone from time to time.

'Your mum had a habit of thumbing a lift home at night,' Caroline went on. 'I often pleaded with her not to do it, or one day she would wake up dead. It was like a joke between us.'

'Was Mum a prostitute?' Sonia asked.

'No,' she replied. 'It was normal to go out, see a guy you fancied and then take him home. Sometimes you'd see him again, sometimes not.'

It sounded a lot like how I'd behaved in my twenties. Sometimes these men would leave Mum some money, knowing she had little, but that wasn't prostitution. Occasionally, Caroline said, she would come back to our house and play music with Mum.

'When she was in drink she could become a little vicious,' she said, 'but she idolised the four of you. When her and your dad separated there was no way she was going to let him get you.'

Hearing this, I thought how she would have turned in her grave when Dad got custody of us.

'On the night she died we were supposed to meet up,' Caroline went on. 'But I'd been persuaded to go night fishing with my ex-partner. I heard that a woman's body had been found on a field in Scott Hall. I said, "Please don't let that be who I think it is."'

Mum's ex-boyfriend had been released from prison a week earlier. He'd served six months for violence towards her. Before his court hearing he'd approached Caroline and Mum and said that if he got time he would kill them both. Initially Caroline had thought it was possible he'd carried out his threat. She waited all day for the woman's name to be announced. When she eventually discovered it was Mum she was distraught.

'Your mum was a lovely woman,' she told Sonia, 'and she knew what she wanted.'

Sonia vowed to start thinking about what it was that she wanted from life. It always filled me with hope when I heard her talk that way.

After I appeared on Radio 4's *Woman's Hour* to promote the book I was contacted by a coordinator who was putting together a conference in the East Midlands for organisations that came into touch with children and families such as the social services, the NSPCC and Sure Start. They invited me to speak at the conference in one of the many workshops. The theme of the conference was 'Hard to Reach Families and Hard to Reach Services'. I accepted the invitation and prepared a talk about my childhood and how I'd been affected.

On the day, Helen came with me to provide much-needed support. By the time I got there the nerves were getting to me and I don't know how I would have managed without her calming me down. I'd written some notes on small index cards to prompt me and within a few minutes of starting I found my nerves had disappeared.

I passed around a photograph of us taken at the children's home as I told my story. I could see shadows of sadness passing over their faces as they looked at it. I went on to describe how Dad had beaten us.

'I'm not going to ask you to picture the sort of thing he often used to hit us with,' I said, picking up a thick, foot-long stick I'd brought with me. I had actually gone out and bought it from the local B&Q, cutting it down to the correct size. 'This was the type of thing Dad used on us. It was a stick like this he used to beat Angela black and blue.'

I swung the stick and slapped my hand, making my palm sting. 'Imagine how it felt on a young child's behind.'

During the questions and answers session afterwards, some-one working for the social services said that such things would-n't happen nowadays. I had my reservations. I was asked what I thought would have helped me back then.

'I think that if I had known through school that what Dad was doing was not allowed and that children were meant to be protected then maybe I would have turned to a caring teacher to ask for help.'

Someone who worked for Sure Start explained that they were discussing whether safe houses on estates would be useful.

'I would have been scared to go to somewhere like that in case someone on the estate had seen me and informed Dad,' I explained. 'Maybe it would be better to have something at school. Then a child could do it in a safe place.'

I felt good when it was all over, and really believed I'd got through to a few people at least.

My appearance on the local BBC news finally produced a response, but not one I was expecting. I opened the letter, hoping that at last we would meet another person whose life had also been completely turned upside-down.

But it wasn't from one of the victims' children. The writer was a man named John Tomey. He had been attacked by a man fitting Sutcliffe's description back in the late 1960s. John was working as a taxi driver in West Yorkshire at the time and had picked up a passenger in the red light district of Leeds. The man had asked to be taken to Bingley but when he got there he had no money and asked to be driven to another address.

We arranged to meet the following Saturday afternoon for a coffee. John was approaching sixty, but seemed to be a man who looked after himself. It was apparent as we talked that he was still affected by what had happened to him all those years ago. He told me how he'd seen the face of his attacker before he had hit him over the head with a hammer from the back of his cab.

He hadn't been able to work since the attack and had mild brain damage, which was obvious when he talked. I could understand everything he said but the words came very slowly for him, taking a lot of effort.

'When Sutcliffe was arrested,' he went on, 'I was convinced I was looking at the picture of the man who had attacked me. I contacted the police to ask if they could check the files to see if any DNA or fingerprints of my attacker were still available to compare with Sutcliffe. But the files had been lost.'

We met again after this and spoke several times on the phone. Although John's experience was very different from mine, this brutal attack had ruined his life. I felt incredibly sorry for him.

chapter seventeen

Hearing
Other Sides

At another SAMM training session in London I met more
people who had lost family members through murder. Both
Kirsty, whose brother had been murdered, and Debbi, a successful businesswoman whose fiancé had been killed in front of her,
had to go to America in order to get the help they needed.

Each was suffering in their own different ways but all appreciated being able to talk freely in an environment where they
wouldn't be judged. I still wanted so much to offer the people in
my area the same opportunity of being with others who understood them and who, no matter what they told us, wouldn't
think they were crazy.

* * *

Another letter arrived from Sutcliffe's doctor, explaining that no visit would be possible due to the amount of media interest in him at the moment. I wrote back directly to Sutcliffe, saying that I agreed but in the meantime I would like him to read my book. I hoped that if he read it I would later be able to invite him to explain why he'd done what he'd done, and to give his thoughts on the effects his actions had had on our family. I felt I needed to at least try to make him think about the consequences of what he'd done.

Sonia was thirty-six now and had been drinking for almost twenty years. She had started having acupuncture and was having another go at counselling, too, attending weekly sessions, which seemed to be doing her some good. Although she wasn't completely cutting out her drinking she seemed to be managing to control it so that she wasn't going on benders, which were the times when she sank to her lowest and when I feared most that she would try again to take her own life.

After so many months of disappointment I finally received a three-page letter from the daughter of another of Sutcliffe's victims. Her story had many similarities to ours and over the next few weeks she sent many letters to both Sonia and me. She didn't want to meet in the beginning, but it was a small step forward and I felt encouraged. At least one of our letters had got through, and had not simply disappeared into a void.

Bit by bit I was making links with others who could help me to change the pictures of the past and to break through the feelings of isolation that I had carried with me for so many years.

Because of the doubts Noel O'Gara had sown in my mind, which lurked despite my conversations with David Yallop, I wanted to speak to Dick Holland, one of the police officers who'd been involved in the investigation of Sutcliffe's crimes. The production company who were making the documentary were able to put me in touch with him and he invited us to his house. I explained I was there to find out about Mum, about what had happened, and about Sutcliffe. Ultimately I wanted to know that the person who murdered my mother was the one behind bars. I told him my suspicions about Sutcliffe's confession, where he said he drove into the car park at the nursery.

'I don't see how this could be true now I've discovered the caretaker's dog was actually outside and just a few metres from where Sutcliffe said his car was parked and where Mum slammed his door,' I concluded.

'Richard,' Dick replied. 'I've been on many murder enquiries, both on the ground and in charge of them, and he [Sutcliffe] is the only killer who removed the knickers just down to pubic hair level. And the stabbing and head injuries were his hallmark, the abdominal stabbing. Now what matters, and what forensics would be tying up, are the circumstances of the attack, not his approach. I don't remember anything on the file about tyre tracks on the approach.'

'He didn't drive onto the grass, just onto the car park,' I said. 'So there wouldn't be any tracks.'

'In the circumstances of the murder, not the overall crime, it doesn't really matter how they got there. What matters is the actual circumstances of the killing assault.'

He seemed to be missing my point. If it wasn't Sutcliffe who had killed my mother then it was extremely important that the way he had said it had happened was unlikely. It threw some doubt on the whole credibility of his confession.

Dick was certain, however, that Sutcliffe had been rightly convicted by the courts for the offences for which he was charged. He even thought there was a possibility he'd committed other crimes that weren't detected. They'd found hammers that matched the exact imprint left on the skulls of many of his victims, although not all. Sutcliffe had even told them where one of the hammers was.

———

After we'd chatted for a while I asked him what Sutcliffe was like. 'When you were face to face with him for a day, did you find him frightening or intimidating in any way?'

'Just the opposite,' Dick replied. 'I thought he was lightly spoken, ever so slightly feminine. An insignificant sort of a bloke. Someone you wouldn't think anything of if you passed him in the street.'

'I imagined him to be a big, towering, overpowering man.'

'No, he was small and he was wiry.'

At the end of the conversation he gave me some advice. 'Richard,' he said, 'you can't turn the clock back in life. All of us have unfortunate things that happen to us. You're at university. I'd make a fresh start. I would forget it. I know it's difficult to forget your mother. You're in a group of people who lost their mothers in tragic circumstances, there are other people who have lost parents in tragic circumstances and you have no alternative but to make the best of it. So try to make a career for yourself so that you're determined to tackle life and say, "My bad start in life is not going to hold me back. I'm getting there."'

I assured him I had every intention of doing exactly that.

Another connection the film crew made for me was with the family of Olive Smelt, who'd been attacked by Sutcliffe a few months before Mum was killed in 1975. I wrote to Olive's husband to enquire if he would ask his children if they wanted to make contact with us.

I received a phone call from Julie, one of Olive's daughters, who said she would like to get to know us. Life seemed to have been just as tragic for her family as ours, even though her mother had survived.

I also found the name and address of Maureen Long, another of Sutcliffe's surviving victims. She too had been left for dead and her life had been affected beyond repair. Like John Tomey she'd received blows to the head, which had left her suffering from mild brain damage. She invited me to her home in Bradford where we spent a few hours reflecting on how Sutcliffe had shaped our lives. A gentle woman, she was slightly deaf and told me she'd been hearing voices of her own. She'd been in and out of hospital trying to get help but the damage seemed to be irreparable.

The more people I met who'd been affected by Sutcliffe, the more I understood how evil he was. I'd read in *Wicked Beyond Belief* by Michael Bilton how he'd been found to be wearing what was described as a 'killing kit', consisting of a jumper which he would wear under his trousers. He would then expose his genitals as his victims were dying and masturbate. What kind of man would find a human being losing their fight for life a turn-on? To me the scene seemed the epitome of evil. More than ever I wanted to get to a place where I could finally put him behind me and concentrate on my future and the good things in my life.

chapter eighteen

Beautiful Roots

In the second week of March the paperback edition of the book reached number one in the charts. I felt it was exactly the sort of memorial Mum deserved.

There is one day every year when I can almost guarantee Sonia will be heavily drunk: St Patrick's Day. I never celebrate it because of its connection with Dad and his drinking. It reminds me too much of his drunken violence as he celebrated his nationality. I truly hate it. I even prefer to forget I'm half Irish because it links me to him. Sonia, however, feels differently. On each 17 March without fail she parties as much as if she were fully Irish herself. This year it was just the excuse she needed to go on a bender, starting a week prior to the day itself.

I was beginning to think Sonia was too far gone, and enjoyed drinking too much, ever to consider giving it up. Her counsellor had explained that she should concentrate on controlling her drinking rather than trying to quit, but that week leading up to St Patrick's Day proved she was far from being able to do that. I just hoped she would get back on top of things again once the day itself was out of the way.

I'd arranged to go up to Scotland with Helen to visit Mum's side of the family the day after St Patrick's Day. I'd decided not to take Sonia as the trip meant so much to me. I was introducing Helen to the family for the first time and I didn't want Sonia to spoil it. When I'd taken her to visit Mum's brother, Norman, and his wife and children in Hull, she drank pints all night and became abusive towards me.

As Helen and I were about to leave I received a text from Sonia: *'Hi. Send my love to all in Scotland.'*

I rang her straight away, thinking she was sober. How wrong I was.

'Where are you?' I asked.

'Going out,' she replied.

It was only three in the afternoon.

'St Patrick's Day is over now,' I reminded her, but she just laughed. I tutted and told her to look after herself.

When I told Helen what state she was in she sighed. In the six months I'd known her she'd seen in me every kind of emotion possible when it came to Sonia; distress, anger, worry, delight when she eventually turned up somewhere sober, and sadness that she was never going to stay on the right track for long. It was part of my life to be thinking of Sonia all the time, trying to help her, worrying about her. Helen was very understanding about it. Six months on and she was still learning more about my family and its history.

In a different way, I was also still finding out more about my heritage, and this trip to Scotland was part of that. We were going to visit the Isle of Skye, where Mum had lived as a teenager.

When I was a child I'd often looked in atlases at the islands on the far west of Scotland and tried to imagine who could possibly live there. There were masses of them and I never dreamed that one day I would travel up there myself.

To break the journey I'd arranged to spend a night with a cousin, Delia, near Edinburgh. I'd met her for the first time at Grandma Newlands' funeral almost two years earlier. We'd kept in touch and I'd stayed with her when I visited the Edinburgh Festival the previous summer.

Many of my cousins on Mum's side had kept in touch, but none on my father's side had ever contacted me. I wondered if it was something to do with the fact that Mum and Dad had separated before she died. Did that exclude us from being part of the family in their eyes? I'd occasionally bumped into them in the street or at a funeral, but not once had any of them visited me or picked up a phone to call me. Now Dad had told me they all wanted nothing to do with me because of the book. So it felt strange to have relatives who actually wanted to know us.

On the drive up to Scotland my mobile rang. I put in my earpiece and answered the call. An old-sounding woman's voice announced that she was Olive Curry. I'd first seen Olive some time ago after she had appeared on a programme about the different women who had written to Peter Sutcliffe over the years. I was thrilled that she'd called me but it wasn't a good time to talk, I informed her, as I was driving. I asked if I could give her a call when I returned. She agreed, telling me she'd thought about me for over twenty years.

My phone went again as we were approaching Edinburgh. This time it was a much younger voice calling from somewhere noisy. It sounded like the type of call I normally received from Sonia when she was drunk and out on the town.

'You don't know me,' she announced. 'I have your Sonia here. She's out of her head and doesn't know who she is or where she lives. Can you come and get her?'

'I'm afraid I'm in Scotland,' I informed her, my heart sinking. I knew only too well what Sonia was like when she was in this kind of state.

'I know who your sister is,' the woman told me. 'Someone in the pub told me about your mum. I run the Three Legs in Leeds.'

It was one of the pubs where Mum used to drink, a place normally frequented by the hardest drinkers. The landlady had put two and two together, knew Sonia had a brother called Richard and had scrolled down the names on Sonia's phone until she came to mine. She'd read my book, she told me, so knew only too well about our history.

The landlady agreed to put Sonia into a taxi and send her home. I gave her Sonia's address, thanked her and hung up. I turned to Helen. 'Is this ever going to stop?' I asked her.

My cousin, Delia, and her long-time partner, Kev, made us very welcome, and we ate and drank into the night. They told us that one of our distant cousins had been looking into our family tree and Delia gave me copies of everything that had been found, including the birth, death and marriage certificates of my ancestors. They'd managed to go as far back as 1760, the year my great-great-grandfather was born.

The marriage certificates stated that many in the family had worked as tinsmiths and that they had mainly lived on the Orkney Isles. I knew already that my grandparents had been married on the Isle of Bow in the Orkneys, in a small place called Flotta. I promised myself that one day I would make the long journey to Flotta to retrace those roots which, until recently, I never knew I had.

The following morning we took the scenic drive from Edinburgh to Inverness, where Mum's three sisters, Lillian, Betty and Iona, lived with their children. Betty's house was going to be our base for a couple of days, and Iona and Betty were there to greet us. Being with her sisters was as close as I could get to being with Mum. I tried to imagine how she would have looked if she'd still been alive.

On the Sunday morning Betty drove us through some of the most breathtaking scenery I'd ever seen. It was like travelling through the Alps, and eventually we arrived at the bridge which connected the mainland to the Isle of Skye. I felt that for a while it didn't matter what had happened to Mum once she'd moved to Leeds, that this was a place where she had been happy. In the years she spent here she was free from all the trouble with Dad and other men, free of the dreaded meeting with Sutcliffe and the years of her face appearing in the newspapers. Living here had been a happy time for her, and Sutcliffe would never be able to destroy that. It was the most remote place I'd ever visited.

The views in every direction took my breath away. As we drove over the recently built bridge, I pictured Mum travelling here by ferry all those years ago.

On the island the coastal route was at times only a single track and we saw the odd abandoned car. On one side of the road the mountains towered above us; on the other we could see smaller islands dotted in the sea.

'Your grandad travelled to Skye nearly fifty years ago,' Betty explained. 'In the early sixties they decided to modernise the track which led north from Portree in the centre of Skye to the small village of Staffin and they needed men to work on the roads.'

We stopped at Portree, a fishing village, and drank in the fresh air. The constant swerving around bends had left me feeling a little under the weather, combined with the champagne we'd drunk at Delia's. We'd been celebrating the paperback reaching number one, and this journey and the celebration suddenly made Mum's death even more heartbreaking.

Sutcliffe had had no way of comprehending where Mum had come from when he killed her. I wanted him to know. I wanted him to realise he'd wiped out someone who had been a young girl once, and went through her teenage years visiting the local highland dances, enjoying the attention she received from the young men of the area. To a girl growing up in such a remote place these dances must have been the highlight of the month. The island was only thirty miles from top to bottom, and eight miles across. It was surrounded by the Atlantic Ocean where seals could be seen playing in the waters. It was a world away from the council estates of Leeds.

'When your mum was around fifteen,' one of my aunts told me, 'our father found her wearing make-up, so he took it and buried it in the garden.'

They told me Mum had always had a bit of a temper and was quite an emotional girl. If she was upset then everyone knew about it. I sometimes felt like this and imagined I'd inherited it from her.

As we drove even further north we passed quaint cottages, all dwarfed by the grandeur of the surrounding scenery. It felt strange to be driving on roads my grandad had worked on. He and my grandmother had travelled to the Isle from a place just north of Inverness, where they'd lived in a log cabin, which Grandad had built with his own hands. It was beside a small stream, Iona told me, tucked away from any passers-by. It all sounded so romantic.

When Grandad had got the job on Skye he'd travelled there with Grandma, Mum and five of the youngest children. Apparently Mum sometimes looked after the young ones if my grandparents were out working.

'I was four then,' Iona recalled. 'Your mum was a teenager and she used to feed us porridge three times a day.'

After we'd been driving around for an hour, admiring the scenery, Betty announced that she 'thought it was here'. I hadn't realised we were being taken to the actual spot where Mum had lived. We drove left down an old track and pulled up. On the right side of the road was a new house and Betty asked the owner, a lady sitting in a deckchair enjoying the sun, if we could climb the fence opposite her house as she owned the land now. 'I lived there when I was younger,' Betty explained.

The lady in the deckchair said it was no problem. There were only three or four other houses in the vicinity and we were around a quarter of a mile from the sea. Betty led the way over the fence and the rest of us followed.

We came across a ruin beside a small loch, which must once have been a stone cottage but was now only chest high. This, Betty informed us, was the house that my mother lived in as a child and, at that moment, gazing at that rugged scenery, the mountains reflected in the water of the loch, I hated Sutcliffe more than ever before.

I wanted the house to be how it was, to be able to see Mum playing in the surrounding fields and on the shores of the loch. I felt so sad to be there, but happy, too. We walked through the doorways and around the inside of what was left of the stone walls, most of which had fallen in and become overgrown by grass. None of us said much. Helen took some pictures of me with my aunts as we stood beside the house.

Before we left I picked up a palm-sized stone from the top of one of the walls and slipped it into my coat pocket as a keepsake. I was beginning to get a very different picture of my mother to the one I had been carrying with me all these years.

chapter nineteen

A New Understanding

'I'm thinking of going into detox,' Sonia said, 'over in Preston.'

It was the best news I'd heard in years. Sonia had broken down in tears and told us she felt she had nothing in her life except alcohol.

'I've been talking to my counsellor and the acupuncturist, and I know that to beat it I have to get away from this area.'

It had never helped that she lived opposite an off licence. Preston was sixty miles away and would give her the chance of a new start. Having heard her say for so long that she wasn't ready to stop drinking, I really believed this was the break-through she needed.

Helen and I left her house feeling full of hope. If she could allow herself to be away from the life she was currently leading for up to a year, some light might finally appear at the end of the tunnel. I also knew from experience that I shouldn't build my hopes up too high just yet.

Olive Curry's story, which she had told on television and in the newspapers, was that Peter Sutcliffe had visited her in the Mission in North Shields, a place where the fishermen and the public could purchase food at reasonable prices. She recalled that when he visited, he was with a scruffy balding man who had remained silent. Olive remembered how, over time, Sutcliffe had told her a few things about his home life, such as his wife's name and that he was buying a home in Bradford.

On one occasion he'd gone out of the room while Olive was clearing the table close to where the pair had been sitting. When Olive asked the scruffy man where his friend was he covered his mouth and looked away from her, mumbling under his breath that he'd gone to the toilet. It sounded to Olive as if he had a lisp.

One day at the end of 1980, a short time before Sutcliffe was arrested, Olive left work at five-thirty. As she did, Sutcliffe appeared from a pub doorway near to where she lived, and approached her. She recognised him and felt a wave of fear she couldn't explain as he came close. Luckily, her son had come to collect her and was waiting on the other side of the street. Olive walked quickly away from Sutcliffe and across the road.

The next day she heard from someone in the pub that a stranger had come in the previous day, causing heads to turn. It was a local pub in which all the regulars knew one another. 'He had a big bushy beard and was dressed all in black. He had an air about him,' one of them told her. 'He just bought himself a pint and seemed to be waiting around for someone.'

Back in those days the pubs shut at three in the afternoon and it seemed likely to Olive that this man was the same person who came out of the pub doorway at five-thirty, and had visited the Mission over the previous months. Olive's son told her he'd seen the dark haired, bearded man appear suddenly as she had approached the doorway, as if he'd been waiting for her.

Neither of them thought any more about the incident until a few weeks later, when the police announced that a man was helping them with their enquiries. Peter Sutcliffe was finally behind bars. When Olive saw his picture on television she recognised him as the man who had been in the Mission. This was the start of her own campaign to make it known that Sutcliffe had visited the North Shields Mission with a friend, who, she reckoned, becuase he was a friend, could possibly be the man who would come to be known as 'The Hoaxer' who had made the tape and written the letters sent to the police in 1978 claiming to be from the Ripper.

(Olive has recently informed me that when she saw a picture of the man arrested for the hoax tapes, he was not the same man she saw in the Mission.)

In her quest to uncover the truth, Olive started writing to Sutcliffe in prison and eventually began visiting him. Like a lot of people, I'd put Olive down as someone who was obsessed and fascinated by him. When I came across an appeal by her for anyone with information with regard to the small balding man, however, I sent her an email, asking if she would like to meet. I gave her my number and waited for her to call, which she had done while I was driving up to Scotland. Once I got back home I made a date to visit her and her friend, Diane Simpson, who had also visited Sutcliffe extensively.

Diane is a highly acclaimed graphologist and the expert who worked with West Yorkshire police on the case. One of her trainees had written a standard letter to a number of pop stars, film stars, politicians and criminals, asking for samples of their handwriting. She'd written to Ian Brady, one of the Moors Murderers, as well as to Sutcliffe.

Sutcliffe had replied immediately and suggested that the sixteen-year-old student visited him. I saw the letter and it was full of charm. He told her he'd read books on graphology, although Diane had copies of other letters he'd written to people in which he said graphology was total rubbish. He was the master manipulator. I didn't read on.

After a few months of corresponding with Sutcliffe, the student fell in love with someone and moved away from the area. At her request Diane sent a compliments slip informing Sutcliffe that he wasn't going to be hearing from her again. Sutcliffe then sent her a reply in which he hinted that he had further confessions to make. Wanting to do the right thing, Diane contacted the police to ask if there were other crimes he was suspected of committing – there were. So she continued with the correspondence and visited him while keeping the police fully informed.

'I've thought about you and your sisters for so many years,' Olive told me when I arrived at her house to see her and Diane. 'But I knew I would never be able to contact you. I just hoped that one day one of you would make contact with me.'

'I thought you might be able to throw light on some of the unanswered questions I have about Sutcliffe,' I explained, 'whether he's sorry for what he did, or has ever shown any remorse. To know that he was feeling remorseful would give us some comfort.'

Olive explained that her only reason for contacting Sutcliffe was to push him for some answers about his visits to the Mission where she worked.

'I always visited with my husband, and even if Sutcliffe had wanted to talk about what he'd done, my husband would never have allowed it.'

Her husband had passed away now and it was obvious she missed him very much.

'I just went along with what Sutcliffe said – and never challenged his defence that he'd heard voices from God – in order to get to the truth about his visits to the Mission.'

Diane, on the other hand, said she did bring up the subject of the children of his victims with him.

'He'd been trying to justify himself about his crimes,' she told me, 'and I said, "You rendered twenty-three children motherless, justify that."'

I could hardly wait to hear what the monster had replied.

'Without a moment's thought he said, "They're better off without their mothers."'

I couldn't believe I was hearing her right. 'We're better off without our mothers? We're better off because our mothers are not here?' How dare he? I thought as I banged my clenched hand onto the table in front of me.

Diane continued. '"Who are you to say that?" I asked. "You don't know them." He worked on the line that these were "bad" women, and the fact that they were out in the evening was justification enough for him.'

He and Diane went on to argue about whether or not our mothers and all the other women had felt anything as they were being killed. Diane agreed with me that of course many of them would have felt something. He described how he had first tried to hit one of his young victims with a hammer, which missed her head and hit his car. The girl asked, 'What did you do that for?' He was then disturbed by taxi drivers, so he pushed her to the floor beside his car. According to his confession he then had sex with her as she lay there. Imagine how she must have felt with his evil face staring at her, knowing he'd just tried to hit her with a hammer, probably knowing that she was looking at the face of the serial killer who murdered his victims with a hammer.

'It wouldn't have mattered who he had come across,' Diane said. 'He would have attacked a vicar's wife.'

'So he's not remorseful?' I said. 'He's not sorry for what he did?'

'He said that the children would probably have been placed into foster care. It took my breath away how easy it was for him to justify what he'd done.'

They'd talked about prostitution and Sutcliffe had said that society was hypocritical in the way it condemned prostitutes and then locked him up for killing them. As I listened I began to understand that he wasn't like your average man in the street with a conscience. He was deranged, self-centred, ill.

'I told him I thought prostitution should be legalised,' Diane said, 'to which he replied, "What, to keep them clean?" I said, "No, to keep them away from people like you." He then stared me straight in the eye and I felt fear. Tears came to my eyes and my knees started banging together, fortunately I managed to control my feelings and changed the subject. When it was time to leave he mentioned my tears and thanked me for being so understanding. He thought I was upset for him and not the poor girl whose death he was describing.' On another occasion when annoyed by something she had said, Sutcliffe blew on the back of Diane's head and said 'Now you've had a blow on the back of the head.' Diane said she didn't want to visit him again but had agreed to continue visiting him at the request of the police in the hope that he could be persuaded to agree to a police interview.

I felt disgusted. He was still frightening women, but now with words.

One of attacks they wanted him to confess to was the case of Tracey Browne, a fourteen-year-old schoolgirl. Tracey had belonged to a youth club and one evening a man was waiting outside. He asked her if 'young Johnny' was around. Tracey told the man that Johnny had already gone. The man pretended to be Johnny's uncle and started walking with her. When she waved him goodbye and turned, he struck her over the head with a hammer four times. He then threw her over a wall, thinking she was dead.

Tracey survived but Sutcliffe never included the incident in his original confession. How could he? He claimed his reason for killing women was that God had told him to kill prostitutes. Tracey Browne was obviously not a prostitute. He later confessed to the attack to Keith Hellawell.

Diane had studied some of Sutcliffe's work records. She'd then compared them with the five hundred or more letters she'd received from him. She showed me a photocopy of two examples of his writing taken from his letters. The first was neat and ordered, calm. The second was a little more erratic. In this letter Sutcliffe was angry and ranting about someone who'd upset him. Diane pointed out that the t's had double horizontal lines on them and there were small marks where his pen had lifted from the paper and left a trail. None of these characteristics showed on the calm letter.

'This,' she explained, 'shows how his writing changes when he's angry. His work records show the same changes in writing. They come in four-day cycles. On the first day there are small changes. On the second day even more and by the third day the writing looked almost like barbed wire. On the fourth day of the cycle Sutcliffe would go out and kill. By the fifth day the writing goes back to normal as though he's released the build-up of tension.' This meant that Mum was literally in the worst possible place at the worst possible time. He was out prowling the streets in a state of tension, looking for a victim, and had come across my mother, whose only crime was that she'd left her children unattended after the babysitter had gone. It didn't matter if Mum was working as a prostitute, whether she was returning home from working in a bar or after a night out. He simply wanted to kill a woman that night and Mum served his purpose.

'This isn't a defence, Richard,' Diane said, 'but he couldn't help it. He's wired differently to me and you. He has a personality disorder.'

I nodded my understanding, realising now that he probably didn't understand why he had killed, any more than his doctors did.

I'd heard enough from Olive and Diane. Peter Sutcliffe didn't deserve my time or the letter I'd written to him, giving him the opportunity of explaining himself. I felt foolish for believing this man was capable of showing remorse or that he would be sorry for what he did. Even if I did hear from him, I wouldn't be replying. I would never fully understand him but now I knew the type of person he was, I wouldn't waste any more time on him. He wasn't important. But my feelings about Mum *were* important, as well as my decisions about the future and Helen.

chapter twenty

A Long-Lost Brother

Alan, Irene Richardson's son, and his wife finally came to meet Sonia and me in Leeds. Helen came, too, to offer moral support, as well as the film crew, which added to the pressure. Sonia and I were very nervous anyway and Alan was running late, having not been to Leeds before. When they eventually arrived I felt as though I was about to have a job interview.

I needn't have worried. As soon as I set eyes on Alan he broke into a beaming smile. His wife gave Sonia a hug while he shook my hand. I then kissed his wife as Alan hugged Sonia. Everyone's emotions were high and the air was electric. The tensions eased as we sat down and started to talk.

'I feel a little intimidated,' Alan said, 'meeting an author.'

'Me, too,' I admitted.

I knew Alan ran his own business and I'd been worried we were going to be from different classes, but I couldn't have been further from the truth. We both agreed we felt like brothers from the first instant. When the filming was over we arranged to go for a meal, away from the intrusive stare of the camera.

'I really appreciate you taking the time to see me,' Alan said.

'It's nothing,' I assured him. 'I just want to help in any way I can.'

I wanted to be there for him if he ever needed someone to talk to. But it was more than that. Somewhere he had a family he'd never met and who possibly didn't know he existed. If I could help bring them together then it was one way of making something positive out of the damage Sutcliffe had done.

When Alan's mother was murdered the police found a photograph of her in her purse, and were able to publish that even before they knew her identity. The article he had been sent quoted a comment from the police, which said something about 'this type of woman'. We wondered how they could have drawn a conclusion like that before they even knew anything about her.

'I want to trace my family roots,' he confided.

It was an urge I could fully understand, since I'd been doing exactly the same in Scotland. I wanted to know where I'd come from and where Mum had come from. It meant a lot to me so I knew how much it must have meant to him with the added distance of being adopted.

It was the day after the Pope had passed away and we went to the church Mum was married in to light a candle and say a prayer. I thought about what Sutcliffe had done to Alan and Sonia and me, and I felt as though there were forces at work greater than I could imagine. Maybe this was a similar defence mechanism to the one that kicked in when Mum died, when I thought she'd been taken as a sacrifice. Maybe the Lord had meant for us to lose our mums for some purpose I couldn't comprehend – or maybe it was just that Sutcliffe really was plain evil.

We went to the shopping centre that housed the nightclub his mum visited on the night she died. As we entered the centre the siren went off and an automatic voice kept repeating, 'Please leave the building.' Alan was very moved, feeling as if his mum was saying, 'I'm here, watching you.'

When we said goodbye it was almost as emotional as our greeting earlier in the day. We vowed to meet again soon.

The day after their visit, Alan's wife texted me in the night, asking me to call as Alan was upset. I got up and rang straightaway.

'I think it's just sinking in that I'm never going to meet my mother,' he explained. 'Until now I've felt as though I'm trying to catch up with her, but now that I've visited Leeds, where she was killed, I've realised I'm getting closer to her but that I'm not going to find her.'

I sat and listened, feeling upset myself. The reality of Alan's pain was brought home to me, more pain that Sutcliffe would never know about, and I was aware that it was just the tip of the iceberg. Helen must have understood what was going on. She made a cup of tea and put it beside me before heading back up to bed. She was great at times like these.

A couple of days later we received news that a place had been found for Sonia at the long-term detox centre in Preston. At last she was taking firm steps to sort herself out.

Two weeks after meeting them, Helen and I made the fifty-mile trip to visit Alan and his family. There seemed to be so many links between us; we each had three sisters, our mothers were both Scottish, we both had partners called Helen and he'd been born eight days before me. Another spooky coincidence was that Alan's birthday was 30 October, the same day Mum was killed.

In one of the magazines that ran a story when *Just a Boy* was published, Alan's mother's picture was accidentally used instead of Mum's. Now I was helping him find his family by telling his heartbreaking story on the documentary. So far my search for the other children hadn't come to much, but I hoped the publicity we were going to gain once the programme was aired would encourage others to come forward.

Although we had a good time with Alan and his family, the weekend did not go as smoothly as I had hoped because Sonia got drunk and we fell out. She sent me a text message telling me to fuck off. I was really disappointed. Things had started to look so hopeful.

The next week I would go back to university. It had been an eventful Easter break.

chapter twenty-one

Good Results

After *Just a Boy* was first published, I was contacted by a woman called Sara. She'd read the book in one sitting and wanted to tell me how people do, and did, care very much about the victims and their families.

'Soon after Sutcliffe was caught,' she told me, 'I saw a handwritten poster in the window of a shop which was under renovation. The builders had put up a poster saying "Let the Ripper go free". I complained strongly to the men in the shop (to put it mildly), and the story was featured in the local paper.'

Sara had worked for many charitable organisations over the years and was now making a film for Refuge, a national charity for women and children experiencing domestic violence. The film was to be used to show how domestic violence can affect people not usually thought of as sufferers and she asked if I would give a man's perspective. The film was going to be used for the probation service, social services and of course Refuge itself.

Eventually I travelled to Bristol to be interviewed. I was asked to explain how it felt to grow up in a family where there was a constant fear of violence from a parent, and how it felt to be an outsider. For the main part I only reiterated what I'd written about and I didn't find it upsetting. I also explained how some of what I had been through was still affecting me today.

For example, I have come to realise that, for many years, I have felt a fear of men, but it wasn't until I met Sara in a bar the night before the filming that I saw the relevance of my behaviour. When we went into the bar, almost subconsciously I glanced round to see who was in, looking out for drunken men, or anyone who might have been expressing any signs of violent behaviour. Sara and I discussed it, and agreed that it was as if some survival mechanism in my brain was on the lookout for danger and ensuring that I stopped well clear of it.

I reflected how for years it had been the same, how I would quickly ascertain that a place was safe, or at least looked as though it was, before going in. I questioned whether or not this was caused by the way we were frightened of Dad, always searching his behaviour for signs of drunkenness or anger. Or was it due to the fact that I had worried as a child that Mum's killer was out there and could possibly be after me? It was perhaps a mixture of both.

Caroline and I had talked about how in my earlier years I'd started to behave a little like Dad. I'd once threatened to throw an ex-girlfriend out of a seventh-floor window in a block of flats. I was ashamed of behaving like that, but there was no point in denying it.

From time to time you would hear about another family in which the children were being neglected or the child had been killed after months of violence. I felt that we were still far from living in a world in which children were safe. We had a lot to learn and this was the reason I didn't hesitate in being involved in something which may help in making people aware of the effects of violence from a parent.

I believed the way Sonia was repeatedly drawn to violent men was another result of suffering at the hands of Dad for so many years. I felt she was still paying for the mistakes social services had made by putting us into Dad's care, and only now, years later, were they funding a rehabilitation programme to deal with the issues that drove her to drink. It was my opinion that if they had done their job correctly in the first place then she wouldn't have been in the state she was today.

* * *

Helen and I had talked about where we were going to go on holiday during May when she had a week booked off. We had both loved Skye so much we decided to find a cottage there for a week over the Internet. I was very grateful that Helen didn't mind holidaying there, as she knew the place meant so much to me. She even bought a mountain bike, and I took mine, so we could enjoy the island together at a leisurely pace.

Sonia's long-overdue journey to recovery was about to begin. She'd been drinking for around twenty years and I knew that if she continued it would kill her. I often feared she would meet her end being attacked after a drinking binge, or that she would be successful in one of her suicide attempts. She put herself in so much danger by allowing herself to be out of control so often. I'd recently given her two books about drinking. They were stories about alcoholics and their recoveries and I thought they might give her hope.

The staff at Preston asked her to go five days without a drink before going in, which she managed to do. When we arrived we discovered the premises was a refurbished church, complete with a spire. It was as if she was entering a spiritual place, being looked after by God. I hoped the atmosphere might give her some added strength.

Sonia's daughter, Leanne, and Helen came with us and we were all shown round together. Sonia was given a room of her own, which didn't have a television. There was a day room where the other recovering alcoholics could mix. Part of the programme entailed socialising with one another, and there were almost daily one-to-ones with a key worker, where they would go through Sonia's whole life.

It seemed that she was in a safe place at last and the plan was for her to remain there for a full year. It almost felt as though she was going to prison as she was going to have a similar amount of contact with the outside world as I did when I was inside. I really hoped that after all this time we'd got Sonia to a place where she was going to get what she needed. Only time would tell.

On 1 May the *Sunday People* ran a headline about the Ripper wanting to kill himself, which I found upsetting. My initial reaction to the story was that I didn't want him to kill himself because I wanted him to remain in prison and serve the rest of his life behind bars. I rang Alan. Once I'd got over the shock I remembered that I couldn't trust the newspapers and that it was probably just a story cooked up for the sake of it. It was still upsetting to have to be reminded of him yet again, but not like it used to be. Even though I'd said it often enough, I felt in myself that I was truly, finally moving on.

It was a bank holiday that weekend and as Helen was working I decided to pop round to see my sister, Angela. As I pulled up at her house my mobile phone rang. It was the daughter of one of the other Ripper victims from the list the private investigator had given me. I'd written some time ago and we had been writing to each other, but this was the first time she'd called. I was taken by surprise. I was nervous all of a sudden and lost for words, but we arranged to meet a couple of days later. I wished Sonia was around as the two of them had become good friends through their letters.

Lisa and I met two days later at Starbucks near Leeds. I felt instantly at ease in her company. We sat for two hours discussing our lives, which had some amazing similarities. She felt the same as I did every time she saw Sutcliffe's picture in the papers. The difference between us was that she'd been brought up by a family that showed her love and made sure she didn't go without anything. It felt good to make another connection with a fellow sufferer.

* * *

Before Sonia had gone to Preston, she, Leanne and I were invited to the television studio to see a private screening of the documentary for the first time. We sat together in a small darkened room. It was very emotional for me to watch, especially the parts where Sonia was alone, which I hadn't seen before.

She was happy at one point because she'd heard from the daughter of another of Sutcliffe's victims. They'd chatted on the phone and as Sonia talked about it afterwards she was the happiest I'd seen her for years. She ended the piece by describing how the woman had said her name. She then spoke directly to the camera, repeating 'Sonia', as though she was over the moon that someone had actually called her by her name. 'It was lovely,' she said, 'it was lovely.' She sounded so sweet and happy and I had to fight back the tears as I watched.

Another scene that moved me was filmed in her kitchen after she'd heard about Sutcliffe's plans to get himself released. Sonia stumbled out of the kitchen, obviously half drunk. It was pitiful. I felt sorry for her, knowing the whole world would see her like this. She had already decided to go to Preston by this point, but I also hoped that this film might be the extra incentive she needed once she arrived. We don't usually get the chance to see ourselves drunk and for the first time Sonia would see how she appeared to the rest of the world.

I hoped too that now Sonia might also be understood a little more and would not be seen as 'just some drunk', but as someone with feelings. I desperately wanted other people to see the Sonia that I knew.

I was unhappy when we first saw Mum's naked body on the screen. I thought hard about trying to get the programme makers to take it out, although I was aware I'd signed a contract in the beginning, which gave all editorial control over to them. Eventually, however, I decided that the public, and hopefully the courts, would see just what this man had done to my mother. What he had done to us. I even hoped it would lessen Sutcliffe's chances of being released.

After we'd watched the documentary for the first time I had to return to the studio and record the commentary for it. This entailed sitting in a booth with the film playing and me being directed when to say my lines. It took many attempts at each sentence to get it to sound natural, and each time they had to rewind the footage in order for me to come in at the right point. This meant seeing the same images again and again. 'It was lovely,' Sonia kept repeating in front of me, and I struggled not to break down.

I felt that at last I was standing proud and talking about the person who had given birth to me. I had that right and if I wanted to try and find the others who had lost mothers to Sutcliffe then I could do so. I was no longer a child, and exploring these things made me understand about being an adult. For years I hadn't talked openly about Mum, then I'd been worried about the book coming out, as though I was the one who had done wrong; now I was finally saying that I had an opinion. I had a voice and I was entitled to say what I felt. If I was making mistakes along the way then I would have to deal with them.

When the documentary was screened to the world I was inundated with messages of support and Sonia eventually received around two hundred emails and letters. She may not have been getting any support from Dad, but she was getting endless amounts from people far and wide. It was perfect timing for her. She'd only been in rehab for a matter of days and now she was hearing from so many people that she couldn't keep up with them. It was the same for me.

The response I got from many of Mum's family made me feel sure we'd made the right decision. They were all behind me and told me I'd done Mum proud. The response I got from the public, friends and family gave me a sense of achievement and I forgot some of the comments I'd made on film which I'd thought sounded stupid.

The programme also produced exactly the right result for Alan. He heard from all three sisters and met up with each of them. He also met many of his Mum's relatives. One of his sisters told him she'd discovered what had happened to their mother twelve years earlier, and was able to tell him where she was buried, making it possible for him to visit the grave for the first time. Another of his sisters got in touch via her social worker. It was great to be able to help them reunite.

I also heard from Jean Jordan's brother, who didn't know that his sister, Sutcliffe's sixth victim, had any children. He asked me to help him find the two nephews he'd never met.

Best of all, I received an email from a woman in London who informed me she had my mother's wedding ring. I almost jumped for joy at the thought of having something that had belonged to Mum, but tried to contain myself until I received confirmation from someone. The woman wrote that she used to be best friends with Vanessa, my cousin, eldest daughter of Mum's sister, Lillian. I quickly sent Vanessa a text message, asking whether she'd ever heard of the woman. She confirmed that she had lived a few doors from them when they'd been in London. She also told me she'd been her best friend while she was a teenager, but that she couldn't remember anything about giving her a ring. It was just under thirty years ago, so I felt it was reasonable for her to have forgotten.

I then rang my aunt, Iona, in Scotland and asked if she knew anything about it. Iona told me there was a chance that it was her ring rather than Mum's – she'd got divorced in 1981 – but I worked out that Vanessa had returned to Scotland by the time Iona had divorced so it probably wasn't her ring. There was a strong chance that this actually was something that had belonged to Mum, something that had been close to her. I decided now to call the lady in London.

She described how, when she was in her mid-teens, she and Vanessa were going through one another's trinket boxes.

'Vanessa said I could have her Aunty Wilma's wedding ring,' she said. 'I remembered being told about how your mum had died and then, when Sutcliffe was caught, I knew it was something I would always keep. I often prayed for your mum and thought about her and the ring every time I saw him on the news. When Vanessa was sixteen she went back to live in Scotland and we lost touch. I saw Sonia and you on the documentary, and I knew I had to return the ring to your mum's children.'

She promised she would send it by recorded delivery to my house and it arrived the next day in a padded envelope. I opened it hurriedly and went to sit down with it. I was startled by how petite it was, and in such good condition. As I sat there looking at it I imagined Mum's tiny finger poking through the gold ring towards me. I then followed her finger in my mind back through the ring towards her hand, up her hand, arm and shoulder until her whole body was there, connected to the ring.

When I was a child, I would sometimes lie in bed, willing her to appear to let me know she was all right, and I found myself doing the same now, wishing that she would suddenly be standing there in front of me, wearing the ring.

The wave of emotion was almost overwhelming. My mother had worn this wedding ring. Her finger had touched what I held between my two fingers and I wasn't able to stop the tears; not heavy sobbing, just tears of sadness. I felt so close to Mum and thought, not for the first time, that she might be looking down, happy this ring had found its way to me.

I decided I would take it with me when Helen and I went to the Isle of Skye for our holiday, and call in at Inverness to see the family, so Iona could try it on. If it didn't fit her then it surely was Mum's ring.

chapter twenty-two

Glimpses from the Past

A number of relatives I hadn't yet met made contact after the television programme. My second cousin, Bunty, who was with my grandparents around the time Mum was killed, described how devastated they both were by the event.

'Your grandma said, "Poor Richard, what will he do without his mum?"' Bunty remembered. 'I told her she'd better get on the phone and insist that the family would have the four of you, but they told her your dad had said he was having you.'

Rose Anne Williams, who was Mum's cousin and knew her until she was fifteen, also contacted me, and I heard from a man who was my best friend on the street we lived on when Mum was alive. 'I remember you being there one day and gone the next,' he said. 'No one explained to me what had happened.'

I then heard from a woman who was married to another victim's son. She told me how the murder of his mother had made him a very angry person and that he was unable to talk about what had happened. She also told me he felt ashamed because of who had killed her, as he felt the public thought all of the victims were prostitutes. The marriage inevitably failed.

I also received an email from a woman who had drunk in the same pubs as Mum. 'Reading your book,' she said, 'and the part where you say they called your mum a prostitute, if that had have happened to any of the women who drank in them pubs, that label would have probably been given to any one of them, even though knowing and being one of the lasses who drank there, the women obviously were not.'

It felt strange to be sitting exams for the first time in my life, nineteen years after leaving school. A lot depended on them because I needed good marks to go on to the Social Policy degree.

The day after the exam Helen and I packed our things and headed north for our holiday on Skye, once again stopping off at Delia's house to break the journey. We were up early again the next morning and off on our journey through the

Cairngorm mountains, past Ben Nevis, eager to see those beautiful views again.

This time we were travelling alone and the more time I spent with Helen the surer I became that I'd met someone really special. She was always there to support me in whatever I was doing and here she was again, willing to make the long journey to the place where Mum had lived. It wasn't her mother but she knew how much it meant to me so she made no complaint about not being able to spend her holiday stretched out on a hot beach somewhere. I loved her for being as enthusiastic about it as I was.

I'd always believed I would know when I came across a woman I felt I could spend the rest of my life with, and with Helen I was becoming more and more sure she was the one for me. I knew that when the chips were down she would be there, no matter what. A few weeks before the holiday I'd considered asking her to marry me but, after a lot of soul-searching, I decided the time wasn't right. I wanted not just the time, but also the place to be the most meaningful possible. I didn't just want to pop the question over a drink in some bar somewhere, and the possibility of asking her on Skye was beginning to seem attractive.

In the end I decided not to do it on Skye. Firstly, Helen had mentioned that if I ever did propose to her she didn't want me to do it on any anniversaries linked to Mum, like her birthday or the night she died. I could see she had a point; we didn't want what was going to be an important day in our lives to be linked to something that might stir up painful memories for me. Skye was a place that reminded me of Mum, rather than being somewhere that was special to Helen and me. It was also only eight months since we'd met and I was a little worried people would think we were rushing into it.

We joked, although deep down we both meant it, that when we had children we would bring them back to Skye to see the beauty and experience a little of their family's history. Between us we would be able to tell our children a lot of stories, with Mum's family coming from the Orkneys and living on Skye, and Helen's mother being Polish and her dad English.

We were always talking positively about our future, as if it were simply a matter of time before we were married and on the journey to becoming parents. Often, when we walked together I would say, 'Come on, you two,' looking behind us as though we had two young children in tow, and would stretch out my hand towards an imaginary child.

Helen thought it was endearing and kept telling me I was going to be one of the proudest fathers. She was right, although at times I feared I would repeat Dad's behaviour. They were only fleeting worries, though, and were quickly banished. I knew I was a different person to Dad; that I was constantly trying to put things right, and to heal the damage done in the past. I'd never once heard of Dad trying to put things right. He always saw himself as the victim. I'd worked hard to understand enough about the past and myself to realise that I would only continue to be a victim if I let myself be one. Now I had a shot at the 'normal' things that I had thought were out of my reach, such as marriage, kids, love, happiness, respect, security and peace. So many people decide to remain victims all their lives.

Helen and I eventually arrived at Uig, a beautiful port on the west coast of the island where the ferries left for the Outer Hebrides. We drove a few miles north to the Steadings, some newly renovated sixteenth-century buildings, which were to be our base during our stay.

We spent the week visiting the island's attractions, starting with another visit to Mum's old house. We couldn't believe how free of crime the island was. People left their houses unlocked and some even left the keys to their cars in the ignition. We tried to imagine living in a place like this but eventually decided we would be too far from the world we knew, from our friends, relatives and jobs.

We cycled, walked and drove all over the beautiful island, not even caring when it rained. What I would really have liked would have been to come across someone who'd known my grandparents, or possibly even Mum during the couple of years she was at school there.

I didn't quite have the nerve to knock on the doors of houses close to hers and ask if they knew the family who had lived in the house all those years ago. Maybe one day, but at the moment it was all still too new to me.

On the last day of the holiday we were passing the ruins of Mum's old house, almost as if we were popping over to say goodbye to her. It was around six in the evening. As we drove north on the narrow road, the clouds started turning black and it looked as though it was about to rain. As we approached the loch close to the old ruin, a brilliant white beam of light broke through the dark clouds, shining down on the side of the hill about two hundred metres to the left of Mum's ruin. I stopped the car, thinking it would make a lovely picture. As I held the camera to my eye I noticed that the beam of light appeared to fall behind and around a small white house. We joked later that we should contact the owners of the house and give them a blow-up of the picture. We then drove past Mum's house and headed inland to our cottage for our last night.

* * *

On the way home we stopped at my Aunty Betty's house again, and went into Inverness town centre to meet up with Iona and one of her friends. I showed Iona the ring that I hoped was Mum's. She took it from me and tried to put it on her finger. It was far too small.

'There's no way it's mine,' she said, and that was the confirmation I needed, although ever since receiving it I'd felt sure it was Mum's anyway.

We had a good night out with them, visiting a couple of the local bars, and Helen even got me to stand up and make a fool of myself singing karaoke – that's how comfortable I felt in her company. Betty, Iona and their friends wanted to go on to a third pub but we decided we'd had enough to drink as we had a long journey ahead of us in the morning.

As we made our way back to Betty's house in a taxi, chatting about what a great week it had been, I noticed I didn't have the ring any more. I'd kept it in my pocket all night and now it was gone. I yelled in horror and asked the taxi driver to stop.

'Helen, I've lost the ring,' I said. All of a sudden it felt as though my world had fallen in on me. The most precious thing I'd ever owned, even if it had been only for a few days, was gone. I was ashamed of myself for being so careless.

'We'll have to go back to the pub,' I told the driver, but which of the pubs had I dropped it in? They were both rowdy places. It was going to be like trying to find a needle in a haystack.

Just as the driver was turning round, I felt the ring, lying under me on the back seat.

'It's OK,' I shouted. 'It's OK.'

The weight left my shoulders immediately, but those few terrible seconds had made me realise just how important that small link to my mother had already become.

In June I sat the final exam of the year. I just needed to pass this one to get onto the degree programme. It was law and criminology, the toughest subject so far. I answered a question on the appeals procedure and had to pick one subject to discuss. I chose prostitution.

I still found it difficult to hear the word prostitute, let alone write about it, without thinking of Mum, but it was a subject I'd given a great deal of thought and research to over the years and I was determined to face my phobia about it.

I believe prostitution should be legalised and made safer. It is a business that has been with us for thousands of years and will probably remain for many more. For many women it's a case of survival, bringing money into poverty-stricken homes, in most cases due to a lack of support from fathers. Girls who are coerced into prostitution by violent pimps, of course, need help to break free. Creating safe zones would also take prostitution away from residential areas, to avoid the problem of non-sex workers being accosted by men looking for trade.

It's a complex subject, but I believe that if it had been legalised and this country had accepted it like other European countries, many of Sutliffe's victims would still be alive now. For years we've read stories of prostitutes being found murdered and these crimes might not have taken place if the women were not walking the streets and were working in safe, legal establishments where someone was looking out for them. Of course, for many of Sutcliffe's victims it wouldn't have mattered what the situation was with regards to prostitution as many were not sex workers and some of those who were may only have been opportunist ones.

I have no issues with most of the men who visit sex workers, as long as the workers are doing it of their own free will and the men treat them with respect and are not violent in any way. I believe there will always be a need for many men to seek the services of sex workers.

I also understood the criminal procedure and had had first-hand experience after what had happened to me in 1997, when I was convicted of the drugs offence. I had been pressured into buying E's for someone who was working for the police, which was nothing short of entrapment and made a mockery of my arrest, but it was too late to do anything about it now. It made me wonder how many other people had been set up and entrapped, and maybe had ended up taking their own lives as a result.

After the exam I felt the pressure lift. Now all I had to do was wait for my results.

Helen and I were invited to Alan's house to celebrate his son's first birthday. I felt quite jealous of him for having a family of his own, but was beginning to believe that one day we would have the same.

It was quite a difficult day for Helen as it would have been her dad's birthday, but once again she was there with me.

Several times during the party I watched Alan on the phone to his newly found sister and I felt proud to have played a part in getting them together.

chapter twenty-three

The Proposal

Helen had told me she wanted to visit the spot where her father's ashes were scattered. He'd requested the same spot where his mother had hers scattered, at the edge of the Peak District at a beauty spot called Toad's Mouth, in an area called Fox House. Its name, Helen told me, came from a prominent rock formation in the shape of a toad, with a clearly defined mouth.

When I woke up that morning I'd made a decision that I had been going over and over in my mind for months. As I set out from my house I texted Helen to let her know I was going to be a little late, and drove to Meadowhall, a large shopping mall in Sheffield, in search of a jewellers. I knew the type of ring Helen liked, something quite contemporary, and I'd made a point of memorising her size after going on a shopping trip with her a few months before. I bought the ring and slid it into my pocket as I headed to her house. I wanted it to be a total surprise.

When we reached the spot I could understand why Helen's family had enjoyed visiting such a beautiful place. It was full of walkers enjoying the glorious scenery from beside a small stream. We stayed for a few minutes before Helen wanted to go back to the roadside to show me the toad-shaped rock.

'We should go back and sit on the rocks,' I said, 'and have a minute's silence.'

I thought about Helen's dad looking down on his daughter as she sat there with me. I wished he'd still been around so that I could have got to know him. I also thought Mum might be looking down, too. After what I imagined was a minute I turned to Helen.

'It's a shame your dad's not around,' I said.

She just nodded, her mind more on the view than me.

'But this is the next best thing,' I went on, gesturing at the beautiful scenery surrounding the spot where her father's ashes were scattered.

She looked puzzled as I knelt down in front of her, still not understanding what I was doing. I nervously pulled the ring out of my pocket and took hold of her left hand.

'Will you marry me?'

I knelt there, waiting for my words to sink in, but she didn't reply. She just kept looking down at me, smiling.

'Of course I will,' she said finally.

A wave of emotion swept through my whole body as the enormity of what we had just agreed sank in. We both burst out crying, wrapping our arms around one another. I didn't care who was looking. All that mattered to me was the woman in my arms and the commitment we'd just made to one another. I'd found a great woman and I never wanted to let her go.

Eventually we let go of each other, drying our eyes and trying to make ourselves look half decent. Helen assured me she really hadn't been expecting it at all. We were walking on air and spent the rest of the day telling Helen's family and friends. When I rang Sonia she was as excited as we were. She'd been telling me to do it for a few weeks, tongue in cheek. I hoped that as an added bonus it would be good for Sonia to be involved with something as normal as her brother getting married and, hopefully, one day starting a family of his own. I wanted us all to move on together to better things.

An email arrived from a reporter on *The Sunday Times* in Scotland, who had been to a preview of shows that were coming to the Edinburgh Festival. She asked for my comments on the fact that someone had decided to write an opera based on the crimes of Sutcliffe. I was disgusted by the idea, even though I had heard about it a few months earlier from Diane Simpson, who had forwarded me an email Olive Curry had received from the author.

He introduced himself as Philip Pywell, and said that he had been researching the Yorkshire Ripper murders and attacks. As part of his research he'd composed an opera on the subject, in Latin. He admitted that he had been asked to leave his Masters program, and put it down to the fact that his work was too controversial for the authorities. He wanted Olive to have a look at the scores and give him some feedback. The story, he said, centred around the hoax tape and Sutcliffe's confessions, and was all about the "fear that was felt by the women, the members of the public as well as in the Police Force". He said he was dedicating the work to the victims.

The opera was going to be performed at the Edinburgh Fringe, and a percentage of the money made by ticket sales would be donated to the victim support group. He promised not to portray the murders "in a vicious way" on stage, he said there would be nobody running around "re-enacting the scenes from the real events". He said it would have been "Brechtain Truth but tasteful!!"

At the time I thought there was a strong chance it would never happen and decided not to worry about it until I had to. But when I heard from *The Sunday Times* that the author was going ahead with it I started discussing it with the members of other families who were affected by Sutcliffe. All of us were in agreement that it was distasteful and that although he'd said it was dedicated to us, we most certainly did not want him to go ahead.

We wrote to tell him our feelings and he replied, assuring us it was not his intention to cause pain or to distress us. He explained that the opera had begun as an academic piece while he was studying for his degree, during which time he had come to know the victims as people. The more he read in the media about Sutcliffe getting on with his life, the more enraged he felt about those who he had killed.

Once again he assured me that there would be "no graphical, distressing re-enactments within the opera". On the contrary, he said, he had tried to empower the women through song. The opera, he explained, would run like a concert of arias. Some of the victims' faces would be portrayed through digital imagery, stating only their names. He then said that Sutcliffe himself would not appear on stage and would not be glorified in any way.

I still wasn't happy, but when I was contacted by some local radio and newspaper reporters I decided not to comment. I didn't want to add any more fuel to the fire.

* * *

I was becoming used to receiving letters and emails out of the blue, but at the end of June I received one which truly amazed me.

Hello, Richard and Sonia

It's taken me some time to find you but here I am. My name is Dugald Ross and I live at 6 Ellishadder, near Staffin, Isle of Skye. As you may be aware, your mother lived at this address with her parents and some of her siblings around 1962–3. Although I was only about six at the time, my older brothers and I have very fond memories of Wilma, simply because she was kind to us nippers; indeed our late parents often spoke highly of her for that and other qualities that are usually absent in teenage years. They also were deeply saddened to learn of her death.

I still recall the day that George Newlands arrived at our family house (next croft to no. 6) and engaged in conversation with my father, none of which I understood due to the fact that Gaelic was my first language. It transpired that he was to be employed as a foreman with Baxters, who were contracted to bring mains water to some of the crofting townships of Staffin, and he wished to rent an empty cottage (no. 6). This was agreed and some time later the Newlands moved in. I also recall Iona

- the youngest? - and some of your uncles, including Norman, Isaac and Raymond. I seem to recall older brothers who visited from time to time during the water contract and who were given temporary employment.

That period was quite an eventful time for us as we followed the workmen and machinery around the crofts after school hours; the Newlands kids often accompanied us to the local school, which was then Staffin Junior/Secondary.

It seems strangely surreal for me to be sitting here in the same room in which Wilma lived and to find myself writing to her son and daughter under what will forever be painful circumstances, but I sincerely hope that you both find the solace that has eluded you for a large part of your lives.

Feel free to get back if you so wish.

Best wishes

Dugald Ross

I couldn't believe that we had been looking at the wrong place all along, but I was also excited since this meant that the house Mum had lived in was still inhabited, and by someone who had known her as a child. I quickly replied to Dugald and told him how we had been looking at the wrong house. He said that he would take a picture of the real one for me and send it by email attachment.

When the email arrived I had to pinch myself. It was the house I had taken a picture of back in May, the one with the beam of light shining down on it. I felt as though Mum had been trying to tell me something.

We sent a few emails to one another, and Dugald invited me to pop in and see him and the house when I was next up. I couldn't wait to make the trip again.

chapter twenty-four

Getting Results

I received my results from the university in June. I'd been awarded 65 per cent, or the equivalent of a 2:1. I was elated. I felt as if I had made it over the first hurdle. The next was to get a good degree before I thought more about which conversion I would need to become a child psychologist, which I was still considering. I was also thinking about being a bereavement counsellor now that I'd come into contact with so many of Sutcliffe's secondary victims, as well as other members of SAMM.

On 18 June the *Sunday Mirror* reported that Sutcliffe was into his third week of hunger strike and that doctors were asking for permission to force-feed him to keep him alive. My feelings were still fluctuating, but on balance I now felt that if Sutcliffe wanted to take his own life then he should be allowed to. He was never going to show any remorse, so what were they keeping him alive for? If he was ready to meet his maker then I was happy to see him go. Maybe Mum and all the others he killed would be waiting at the gates to greet him and we would be able to put him behind us once and for all. After Diane Simpson, the graphologist, explained her four-day-cycle theory I had come to realise the murder wasn't personal. Mum could have been anyone. On 30 October 1975 he had just needed someone to kill.

The people promoting the 'copy-cat theory' were becoming quite aggressive towards me when I didn't completely back them up, one even calling me 'the son of a whore' in an email. I was starting to accept that I may never know the complete truth of what Sutcliffe did, but that he was probably guilty of the crimes he was convicted of, and maybe many more.

Newspaper reports still have the power to disturb me and I had a particularly scary nightmare one night, in which Sutcliffe chased me down the canal beside the high school I went to, the same canal I once almost drowned in. He was taking shots at me with a gun from the opposite bank.

Eventually the tables were turned and he was strung up, bound by a rope, hanging from a metal beam. He was swinging from side to side and two men were throwing punches at him as he swung close to them. The next thing I was close to him and I had metal spikes in the soles of my shoes. I was slightly higher than him so I could tear away at the skin on his face. Maybe I was sick of still seeing his picture in the papers and I was trying to disfigure him.

Whatever I was thinking, I woke up in a sweat. Helen was beside me and asked what was going on. Even in my half-asleep state I knew not to spoil her night by mentioning him.

'I'll tell you in the morning,' I said, holding her close as we both fell back to sleep. Thank God I had her now and knew that she would always be there for me.

On 1 July Sutcliffe was back in the papers. The story was that the infamous hoax tapes and letters, which could now be tested for DNA, were reported to be lost. Once again it seemed the West Yorkshire police had made a hash of the investigation. At the time the hoaxer had thrown the investigation into Mum's killer completely off track, with the disastrous result that three more women had lost their lives because the police were looking for someone with a Geordie accent. When I visited Olive Smelt, who had been attacked by a man answering Sutcliffe's description, she told me that she had always known that the hoaxer with the Geordie voice was not the man that attacked her, so could not have been the Ripper. She said the police would not listen.

(In October 2005, I was shocked to learn that a man had been arrested for sending the tapes and letters, which had after all been located. John Humble was convicted of perversity the course of justice and received an eight-year sentence in February 2006.)

Later in July the *Sun* announced that Sutcliffe had been devastated by the death of his younger sister. Anne Sumner had died at the age of fifty-six, after an eight-month battle against cancer. He finally got the news of her death through staff at Broadmoor.

Apparently this was a great blow to Sutcliffe, coming so soon after the death of his father the previous year. He claimed he was closer to Anne than any of his other brothers and sisters. He turned to 'comfort eating', bringing himself to the verge of a diabetic coma. After bingeing on sweets and biscuits, his weight ballooned to seventeen stone. He then went on hunger strike leaving his health in an even worse state.

I had another dream in which I was in a prison cell with Sutcliffe. It was an open cell with four beds on each side, similar to the wards in the hospital wing of Armley prison. I went over to him as he lay on the bed, and jumped on him with both my knees on his neck. I shouted that I was going to rip his brain out and feed it to him. (I think I must have got this from a Hannibal Lecter film.) I then jumped off him and he got up from the bed, smiling, and took a microphone from under his top. It was connected to a cassette recorder. He'd taped the threat and was going to use it against me. Then all the other inmates helped me to set about him, smashing the cassette player and unravelling the tape so it couldn't be played.

I guess my mind is still struggling to let go of the fears.

I contacted the Youth Offending Service and asked if they would consider me as a session worker. This kind of work was relatively new and was an attempt to nip offending in the bud by the way of restorative justice or work in the community. If an offender had defaced a bus, for instance, he would be asked to wash buses, if he had damaged some property he would be asked to tidy the gardens of the elderly. I told the person in charge that I had a drugs related conviction in the past but that I'd turned a corner and wanted to do whatever I could to help others.

'If I can show someone that there is another way,' I said, 'then I'll be doing something useful. And maybe I could understand some of the complexities of their lives and perhaps stop someone from going down the wrong road.'

I was interviewed and asked to fill in an application. Then I was told once again that I would have to wait to hear.

* * *

Leanne and I drove to Sonia's rehab centre in Preston to attend a support group for residents' families. It was great to be with others who knew exactly what we'd been through. We were one of the newest families and it was encouraging to hear the others talk about how their loved ones were still sticking it out after five, six and seven months. It was the first time Leanne had ever felt able to really talk about her mother's drinking.

It had been a little over two months since I'd driven Sonia there for the first time. Just the thought of getting her to the three-month point was something I wouldn't have believed was possible back then; each day for Sonia was an achievement, but to be thinking about the possibility of six months was a dream. I was starting to hope that this really might be the end of her drinking problems.

Sonia had had a bad week after starting to deal with the issues that had moulded her personality for so many years. Now, without the aid of alcohol, she was realising what kind of life she had had, which was upsetting her. She told me she'd decided to write a letter to our father. Now she could see what he'd done and how it had affected her, she was extremely angry with him.

'Can I read the letter out to you?' she asked one evening on the phone.

Helen and I were running late and I asked if I could ring her at noon the next day. She agreed, but I felt a little bad about putting her off in this way. The next morning I drove to Preston and rang, as promised, at noon, from outside the gates of her rehab. She sounded OK and started to read the letter out.

'Sonia,' I said, 'do you mind if you read it to me when I next see you face to face?'

'Richard!' she replied, exasperated.

'Or I could read it for myself,' I said, 'as I'm parked outside.'

There was a chance she might not have wanted to see me and I was a little nervous she might not be up to visitors because of the bad week she'd just had. I needn't have worried as she screamed my name and put the phone down. I knew it had been worth the trip as she came bursting through the front doors of the church, beaming and throwing her arms around me. It was great. I stayed for a couple of hours and it was just like old times as we sat and chatted. I said I thought it was a good idea to write to Dad to tell him how she felt. I'd done the same. I'd felt I needed him to know what he'd done and Sonia was now feeling the same. But I doubted if she would get the response she was after, if she heard anything from him at all.

The day had finally arrived. A group of people who had lost their mothers to Peter Sutcliffe had decided to meet. It was the culmination of the months of work Sonia and I had put in to tracking these people down and trying to make contact. In a strange way it felt as though meeting up was an act of defiance against Sutcliffe. There would be five of us: Sonia and I, Alan, and two other women, Lisa and Joanne.

Before leaving for the meeting I turned on the television to watch the morning news. Once again the Yorkshire Ripper was on the front page of the newspapers. The presenter picked up various Sunday morning newspapers and eventually came to the *Sunday People*. There was Sutcliffe's face staring out at me yet again. It was reported that he had spent £10,000 on his ex-wife Sonia in an attempt to win her back. I wasn't angry. In fact, I almost laughed at how ironic it was that we were having our first group meeting and he had hit the headlines again.

I drove over to collect Sonia from her home, which she was now allowed to visit for the weekend. She was a little nervous about the meeting and I tried my best to be reassuring. From the look of her house she had spent the whole weekend cleaning the place. It was spotless and nothing like the state it had been in after weeks of binge drinking in the past. We then went to collect Lisa, who met us at a service station near Leeds.

After an hour's drive we arrived at the hotel where we had arranged to meet Alan and Joanne. They were sitting at separate tables as they had never seen one another before. I had no way of knowing what Joanne looked like but as I walked into the hotel bar I knew who she was as soon as I saw her. She had a look of her mother, whose picture I had seen so many times over the years. Her two sisters lived abroad and I had also been communicating with one of them by email. We kissed and I introduced her to Sonia and Lisa. Then Alan and his wife Helen spotted us and headed over. We pulled up a few chairs round a table and I ordered drinks. Non-alcoholic, of course.

We chatted, sometimes with two conversations going at once. We all said how comforting it was to be together after all this time. It was an exclusive club, which no one would wish to be in although we had no say in the matter. Joanne had always wondered how the other children had fared and she was glad I had taken the brave step that had brought us all together. It was great to hear this after having had so many doubts when I first set about looking for others in our position. I hoped our mothers would have been happy that we had met.

After two hours of non-stop conversation I asked if we could take a picture. We all got together on a sofa and had someone take our photograph. I hoped that over the months and years we could grow in number.

As we all stood around, about to say our goodbyes, the alarm in the hotel sounded, reminding me of the time when we had first met Alan four months earlier. Here we were again about to part and were drowned out by the high-pitched alarm.

Alan and I looked straight at one another as if we knew what the alarm meant. Sonia looked at Alan's wife, Helen, thinking the same. We all headed outside the hotel, amazed at the coincidence. Maybe we just wanted to believe our mothers were there looking down on us all. I was prepared to keep an open mind. We all kissed and hugged in the car park and insisted that we should now make this a regular event and that hopefully more would join us. I left the hotel car park feeling warm inside, knowing this was the start of something great.

After communicating with Dugald, the man who was now living in the house Mum and her family lived in for a couple of months when she was a teenager, I made the nine-hour drive to Inverness once more, stopping the night at Aunty Betty's. In the morning I set off for the Isle of Skye alone, excited at being there for the third time in a year.

I arrived at Loch Mealt and immediately spotted Dugald's house across the water. I'd looked at it so many times in the photo. Pulling up, I spotted a man I guessed was Dugald. The cottage was on a sloping hill and beside it his children were playing on what looked like a homemade slide, built out of polythene and covered in water. In front of the house was an expanse of greenery leading down to the loch. It was an idyllic place and I imagined Mum playing in the same garden when she was young.

We went for a walk to the next house, two hundred yards away. Dugald explained how he'd spotted my grandfather walking along the very same track forty-odd years earlier, dressed smartly in his brown pinstripe suit.

For Dugald there was always something going on at the Newlands' house. He remembered Mum vividly and spoke highly of her. On one occasion he had stumbled across an ants' nest and his head had become infested with the insects. As Mum's house was closer he ran there instead of his own home. Mum came to his rescue, filling the iron bath with water and shampooing his head clear of ants. As soon as Dugald got home his mother asked what the strange floral smell was. They'd never had shampoo back then. From what Dugald could remember, Mum always seemed to be helping around the house, although she was only in her early teens.

Dugald's wife asked me to join them for some homemade soup and sandwiches. I felt as though I'd stepped back in time as I sat browsing through his photo album of the old house, seeing how it used to be. Dugald had ripped the old croft cottage down to the gable ends twenty years before and rebuilt the house, but he kept the old fireplace in its original position. He gave me a picture of the living room as it was when Mum lived there. The walls were clad in original pine and it looked a lot nicer than I'd imagined. The chair that my grandad used to sit in was placed in front of the fireplace.

After we'd eaten in the kitchen, Dugald took me through to the lounge where the fireplace still was. I felt so close to Mum, knowing she'd stood in the exact same spot. I turned and looked out of the window at the same view she would have seen. It clearly hadn't altered in all that time, unlike the ever-changing Leeds landscape. Dugald told me how Mum once dropped the hot ashes from the coal fire and some had gone down a small mouse hole. She quickly got some water and poured it down the smouldering hole.

After a couple of hours I said my goodbyes to Dugald and his family. I drove down the path leading to the single-track road and laughed to myself as I passed the ruin we'd visited earlier in the year.

As the Edinburgh Festival was on I decided to go to the infamous opera based on the crimes of Peter Sutcliffe. I wanted to see for myself that Mum and all the rest of Sutcliffe's victims were not being used in any way that would be offensive. My cousin, Delia, and her partner said they would come to support me. I rang the booking line from their house.

'I have to inform you,' the girl said, 'there will be images that you might find disturbing.'

The comment took me by surprise and I couldn't speak for a few seconds. She asked if I was OK.

'What kind of images do you mean?' I asked.

'Pictures of dead bodies,' she replied.

I couldn't believe what I'd just heard. I hadn't thought there would be any need to show pictures of our dead mothers. After a few seconds composing myself I said I understood. I now knew I was right to check out this show. I could already imagine the letter I was going to send to the writer.

We drove the few miles into Edinburgh and found the venue. Arriving early we went for a drink. When it was announced that *Murder in the Heart* was about to start we headed for the door, ensuring we would get good seats. We needn't have worried. There was no one else in the theatre.

My heart was beating, not knowing what to expect. Before any singers came on stage we heard a voice played over the speakers.

'… she was hit over the head and stabbed fourteen times … behind the nursery building …'

I assumed it was supposed to be a news story and was a description of Mum's murder. On a large screen at the rear of the stage appeared a picture of Mum and her name. My heart was racing. Three female singers came on dressed in brown cloaks with masks over their faces. They started to sing in Latin and obviously I couldn't understand a word they were saying. Then a man entered with a claw hammer in his hand, which he raised in the air and brought down.

From the programme we were given to understand that the man was Phillip Pywell, the author of the opera. In his email he'd assured me Sutcliffe would not appear in the show in any medium. The man who held up the hammer had a beard exactly like Sutcliffe and it was this image that was on the cover of the programme.

After watching a few extremely amateur minutes I told Delia I'd seen enough. As we left the singers singing to no one I felt comforted that Pywell's attempt at bringing in the crowds had failed. It was one thing writing about my life, my experience of Peter Sutcliffe and how his actions had affected me and my family, but to try and turn it into something for entertainment was another thing.

chapter twenty-five

Moving On

At the end of the summer Samaritan Volunteers asked me to speak to their annual conference in York. It would be an audience of about two hundred and I said yes without really thinking about it. It was only when I went into the lecture room to ask the technician to load my Powerpoint presentation onto the PC, that I realised the size of it and my heart really began pumping. Banks of empty seats stared at me and I could suddenly imagine them full of faces, all looking down at me.

After lunch I arrived fifteen minutes early, with Mary, my chairperson. We tested the mike and the Powerpoint. The images flicked smoothly up onto the large screen at the front of the theatre. People without tickets kept asking to be squeezed in. We had to turn them away; there just wasn't room. Someone arrived with a copy of *Just a Boy* and asked if I would sign it for her. She was disappointed at not being able to get in. A queue was forming outside and we had five minutes to go. I decided to go to the toilet and get out of the way while everyone took their seats.

As 2.15 approached I walked back down the corridor, as ready as I was ever going to be. Outside the door were more people hoping to get in. I couldn't believe how many were interested in listening to my story.

'You ready?' Mary asked and I nodded.

Walking in through the double doors I was taken aback by how many people had managed to squeeze in. I took a seat behind the lectern and tried to keep breathing slowly. Everyone's eyes were on me. I was petrified. Mary took the stand and said a few words about me. Everyone was clapping and I knew there was no turning back now. I got to my feet and took the couple of steps to the lectern. I thanked everyone for choosing to come and listen to me, as there were six other seminars running at the same time.

'I'm going to start by talking about suicide,' I explained. 'Then I'll be stepping back in time to tell you where it all went wrong, and how my life took an unexpected turn.'

The title of my seminar was *Just a Boy* and I was going to read chapter one to them. I'd been practising it in my bedroom, ensuring I wouldn't become tongue-tied.

'Has anyone here read my book?' I asked, and a number of people put their hands up. 'I'll read a part of it, then I'm going to condense the rest of my story into around twenty minutes and finish off talking about the SAMM organisation. If there's any time left I promise I will answer any questions you might have.'

So off I charged, picking up the book to start reading, before remembering I was supposed to talk about suicide first. I hoped this wasn't a sign of how the rest of my talk was going to go.

I brought up a large picture of Armley prison and talked about the man I found hanging in his cell. I explained how Armley prison had a high suicide rate but how Samaritan Volunteers were doing a great job supporting the listeners on the wings. I told them about my decision to end my life, which came when I was released. I described my suicide pact with Sonia and how she took her tablets later the very same day.

I left them with that thought, then picked up my book and started reading again. I read it as clearly as possible and I felt more and more relaxed as I went. I showed images along the way, one of the house we lived in with Mum, one of Beckett's Park Children's Home, the photograph of the four of us which was taken for the newspapers, one of Mum, and finally I finished the chapter.

I received a massive round of applause and I noticed a few people were crying. I then explained how as a child I had thought about what had happened, how I had feared life itself, Mum's killer and Dad's violent behaviour. I talked about how we were failed by the social services on many occasions; how all of us left home in our teens with no real role model, and how I thought a happy family life should be. I then told the rest of the story, including my time in the army, my breakdown, my involvement with drugs, turning to Samaritan Volunteers, my time in prison and eventually returned to the story of my suicide pact with Sonia. I could almost feel their relief as I explained how Sonia wasn't successful in her suicide attempt and how I had climbed back from the brink and made a better life for myself, kept my house and become involved with SAMM.

The last picture I showed was one of Helen and me. I was proud to announce that the new life I had been seeking since Mum had died had found its way to me and that Helen and I planned to marry the following year. The applause was even louder than before and seemed to last for ever. I thanked every-one and Mary then said that we would now take questions.

Many, many hands shot up and one by one I listened to their questions or comments, all full of praise and many disgusted at the system for continually letting us down. I explained how the previous week I'd received a letter from the social services informing me that no records whatsoever were kept about me. I'd written to them a month earlier to ask if they had a file or any notes on my childhood, trying to find out why they decided to place us with our father and not with any of Mum's family. I told the audience how nothing about the inadequacies of the social services surprised me. Children were still slipping through the net. I could see it all around me. I was thinking of high-profile cases like that of Victoria Climbie, the eight-year-old who was allowed to die of hypothermia by her incredibly cruel and neglectful relatives, and the more recent one of the couple who allowed their children to starve while they played with their electronic toys. But I was also thinking of cases where I had a personal interest and suspected that social services still failed to protect children in many instances.

After half an hour of questions we had to say that was the end. People then came down from the seats to speak to me, to ask me to sign books and to have photographs taken with me. As I walked away from the event many more were stopping me, wanting to thank me for such a moving seminar. I eventually drove back to Leeds, once again fighting back tears.

chapter twenty-six

The Final Farewell

Helen and I decided to throw a party to celebrate our engagement. We wanted to hold it at her house in the garden and kitchen, but needed to make a few changes to make it work. Helen had a window knocked out which faced the enclosed garden at the back of the house and French doors were put in. She then arranged a large decking area, which totally transformed the garden. It was completed the day before the party.

I hired a band I'd heard the previous Christmas. We filled the garden with a hexagonal gazebo, tables and chairs. There was a trampoline and tent for any children who came. We bought crates and crates of beer and boxes of wine.

As we were planning to amalgamate our two houses full of belongings into one when we finally moved in together, we asked people not to bother with the usual toasters and gifts which we would never use, and asked them to bring plates of food instead. We invited around a hundred and twenty people and almost a hundred turned up, kicking off at noon and going on through the night.

On the day the sun shone as brightly as we could have hoped for. We put a fridge out in the garden for people to get cold beers and soft drinks and I wired speakers from the house into the garden. The atmosphere was brilliant. Other than my cousin and her family, none of my family was there. It hurt me but with all the free drink around, and considering Sonia's problems, I'd decided it wasn't worth the risk of inviting her. I needed to be relaxed and happy on what was a special day for me. I didn't want to have to be on guard all the time, wondering what my sister was doing. Helen still hadn't seen her when she was drunk and I didn't want today to be the first time, especially as her mum had been an alcoholic.

As the band arrived and set up their things, I noticed Eileen and Caroline take hold of the microphone. I cringed at what they were about to say but I needn't have worried. They had secretly gone to Helen's family members and friends and found out snippets of information about her, and they already knew lots about me. Eileen then made one of the most wonderful speeches about the pair of us, about our faults, the similarities in our lives and our decision to change direction in recent years. It brought home to me what we had agreed to when I proposed to Helen. This truly was what I wanted more than anything; to marry a woman I was in love with, whom I trusted and respected, and who felt the same about me.

The band played and I was relieved as I swallowed back my tears, glad the focus was now on them and not me. When they finished their first set, all the salsa dancers got up and danced to the salsa music coming through the speakers I'd wired from the stereo in the house. It was a perfect day and one I knew would have almost certainly been spoilt if Dad or any of his family had been there. Although it saddened me, I knew they just weren't part of my life any more. I hoped that one day Sonia would truly be able to conquer her demons, so that she could be fully involved in our future.

Other things began to fall into place. I was finally able to find a room for our SAMM group in the Civic Hall in Leeds and we had a small group at the first meeting. I felt a great sense of achievement. I was also accepted onto the Youth Offending Team in Leeds, working with young men who have slipped off the straight and narrow and have been involved with the police.

I also attended my first university lecture as a proper student. The previous year had all been preparation for my degree and ensuring that I was at the required standard to progress. Now it was the real thing. The subject of this first lecture was the Welfare State and we were to be shown a film about the life of someone at the 'sharp end of the wedge'.

I couldn't believe it when I saw that the film was about an area called Lincoln Green, where I had lived for four years when I came out of the army in the early 1990s. There was some old footage showing Pat Phoenix, the *Coronation Street* star, officially opening the estate in the mid-1960s, followed by a description of how it had now changed to a place where people no longer wanted to live, where unemployment was rife and everyone walked in fear.

I wondered if the rest of the undergraduates watching the film, most of whom came from other parts of the country, would know anything of such places. I knew for certain that no one in that lecture hall would have imagined that just a few years earlier I had actually lived in that very estate. At that moment I realised I'd come a very long way.

Helen and I discussed what our plans were for the future. As my home had only one bedroom it looked as though the sensible plan would be for me to move in with Helen, into her two-bedroom detached house in Sheffield. It was going to be hard driving to and from Leeds each day that I was in university, or had other commitments, but I couldn't expect her to uproot and move.

Helen decided she would like us to marry in the parish where her parents had last had a house together, before they had both passed away almost two years earlier. The church was beautiful and quaint. We spoke to the vicar about getting married the following summer and we finally set a date for 11 August 2006.

Excited, we started thinking about guest lists, which was a worry for me. There would be alcohol at the reception and I knew only too well that there was a risk that one of my family might have one too many and spoil the day. The other disappointment was that I realised it would be a miracle to have any of the McCann family there apart from my sisters. I knew only too well how they felt about me writing the book. I decided I would worry about the guest list a little later. All I knew was we were going to be married and it felt wonderful.

In mid-October Helen and I gave Mum's grave a makeover. We made a border from black edging stones and dug away all the turf. We then laid down polythene and covered the whole grave with small bright white stones.

On 30 October 2005 it would be thirty years since Mum had died. I had finally managed to organise a memorial service for that day, and had invited all of her brothers and sisters. After four months, Sonia was now out of rehab – before the programme had ended – and I hoped she would remain sober.

On the evening of 29 October I didn't want to go to bed. Thirty years ago, Mum had had her last night on the town. I knew she had died around 1.30 a.m. and something compelled me to remain awake. As the hours ticked by I imagined her catching the lift from Sutcliffe, thinking she was heading home to us. When it got to 1.25 a.m. I stepped outside, unbeknown to Helen, who was asleep upstairs. It was cold, dark and quiet as I stood away from the house. I thought about Mum and about what had happened to her at that hour all those years ago. After about fifteen minutes I went inside and up to bed.

The next day I felt as though all the pressure was on me. I'd arranged everything and if it didn't go right I would have felt as though I had let Mum's siblings down. We got there a little early and placed our flowers on the newly decorated grave. I had bought a wreath spelling the word 'MUM' made from white carnations with a pink ribbon border, and Mum's sisters had ordered a large pink heart with a white border. Sonia, Angela and Donna had also brought their own large sprays. They looked beautiful. We headed back to the gate of the cemetery where we were due to meet everyone else.

The bagpiper arrived in full Scottish attire and as the family arrived he started to play the Scottish anthem. There were about fifty of us in the end and we set off slowly to the sounds of the bagpiper. When we reached the graveside I placed the life-sized passport photograph, which my photographer friend Alex had enlarged, against her headstone. For me it was as though she was there with us. We were celebrating her short life and the children and grandchildren through whom she would continue. Sister Brigid, the chaplain from a hospice where Caroline's husband is head of palliative care, said the most wonderful words about Mum. There was a lot of emotion but somehow I was able to hold back the tears. Then I stepped forward and read out a poem called 'She's Gone', which was about what Mum would have hoped for after she had gone, about the positives and about her memories.

The bagpiper played 'The Skye Boat Song' and then it was Donna's turn to read a very moving poem of her own. I couldn't hold the tears back any longer. I didn't look up but I could hear sobbing around me. I pulled myself together as Sister Brigid said a final few words and a last prayer, and the bagpiper played again to end the service. It had been perfect.

I had brought with me a bag of grey pebbles and now I took one from the bag, putting it on Mum's grave. It was a token to symbolise that we were now leaving behind our suffering and old, negative feelings. Sister Brigid asked everyone else to do the same. The grey pebbles we all placed on the grave would be there among the bright white stones for evermore, as a reminder both of a beautiful day and of all those who were there to share it.

Epilogue

A week later we were having dinner with some friends at their house in Leeds and the subject of where we were going to live came up. They suggested that it would be easier for us to live in Leeds rather than Sheffield. I had always thought that this would be the best course of action but I hadn't wanted to put any pressure on Helen to move away from her family. To my surprise, Helen thought it was a great idea. We all got on the laptop after dinner and started looking at houses in north Leeds. We soon realised that it was going to be possible for us to afford a reasonable home if we both sold our properties. I was so glad that I had got on the property ladder when I was twenty-four and that I had managed to save my home when I came out of prison. We could now buy a home that one day we might fill with a family.

Over the next couple of weeks we viewed as many houses as possible. Eventually we walked into a newly renovated semi in a tree-lined cul-de-sac close to Roundhay Park, not far from the house I lived in with Mum. As we approached the house we saw a car pull up at one of the other houses and three or four small children got out. We felt that this street could just be what we were looking for.

The house had an enormous garden and we both knew immediately that it was the one for us. We tried not to look too interested and we arranged for a second opinion from friends of ours. Soon after, we put in an offer and sat back and waited.

The following weekend Helen took me by surprise by asking if we could start trying for a baby now. As she was thirty-eight she felt that it might take months for her to become pregnant.

'Yes, OK then,' I said. I didn't even have to think about it. I knew that I wanted to be with Helen and having children was definitely part of the plan although something inside me kept warning that maybe it wasn't going to happen.

The very next week Helen's period was late. When we got to the end of the week I suggested that we had better get a pregnancy test. We headed nervously for the chemist and found the shelves with the pregnancy tests, feeling like two naughty teenagers frightened of telling our parents. I remembered going through this when I was sixteen with my first girlfriend. That had been a positive result but we discovered that she hadn't followed the instructions correctly and in fact she wasn't pregnant. Now, twenty years later, I was actually hoping for a positive result and we were definitely going to read the instructions this time.

When we got home we sat down on the floor in the carpeted bathroom, cross-legged and facing one another. I had my thumb covering the small windows on the test stick and my watch in my right hand. We would have our result in sixty seconds. We watched the second hand make its way around my watch face. I counted: thirty seconds, twenty seconds, ten, five, four, three, two, one.

'Are you ready?' I asked.

'Yes.'

I slowly moved my thumb down the stick to reveal the first window. The instructions told us that a thin blue line here indicated that the test had been successful one way or another. It was. I took my thumb away to reveal the second window. Time seemed to stand still as the significance hit us both. Two windows, each with a blue line through them, confirmed that we were now parents-to-be. Tears flooded down Helen's cheeks and I could do nothing but burst into laughter. We threw our arms around one another and held each other. The news meant that when Helen and I had discussed trying for a baby a week earlier she had already been pregnant. We got on the phone and it seemed that whoever we tried to tell was either out or their phone was engaged. We decided to announce it to the world the next day.

Our offer on the house was accepted and we were over the moon. As Helen was now pregnant it was obvious we were not going to be able to get married as planned, especially as we realised that the due date was 11 August, our planned wedding day. We decided that we would marry as soon as we got settled into the new house and the baby was old enough to stand. Christmas came and went and in February 2006 we moved into our new family home. It was amazing to have such a big house after living in my one-bedroom home, which I had been so proud of for so long. We both knew that this house was perfect for us and the new baby when he/she finally arrived. The street definitely had a community spirit about it, with neighbours knocking on the door introducing themselves and giving us welcome cards.

As Helen grew bigger and bigger I became more and more proud to be seen out with her. I couldn't comprehend that I, Richard McCann, was going to be a father at last. I had always wanted a family of my own but as the years had passed by and as my sisters all had children, I had begun to worry that it would never happen. The confirmation came when we went for our first scan and we saw the baby do a somersault in front of our eyes.

At the end of May, when Helen was around six months' pregnant, we decided that we would rather have 'Mr and Mrs McCann' on the baby's birth certificate. Helen suggested that we could get married on Skye, which I thought was a great idea. Mum's birthday, on 1 July was looming, and we decided that if it was possible to arrange we would travel up to Skye and get married in the place where Mum had been happy as a teenager. I contacted Dugald Ross and asked for the details of the local priest. I then called him and explained that we wanted to marry as close as possible to the home that Mum had lived in as it meant so much to me. He told me that in order to do this we were going to have to travel up to the parish three or four times before he would agree to it. This just wasn't possible as Helen was struggling with her pregnancy and the 800-mile trip was not something she could manage that many times. We decided that it had been a crazy idea trying to arrange it all so late.

Dugald then told me that in Scotland you could have a civil wedding just about anywhere as long as you obtained the appropriate licence. He offered his home as the venue and I knew immediately that it was perfect. Although the house had been renovated since Mum lived there, the three steps that led up to the door at the front were still the same ones. Helen and I decided that we would marry on those steps.

We didn't tell a soul and we set off on the journey by train as Helen only had six weeks before she was due. The journey was magical. We both knew that we were travelling somewhere very special, to do something even more special. We had none of the usual stresses that come with a wedding because we only had the two of us to think about. When we got to Skye we decided to take the old ferry as Mum would have done when she came to live here for a few years, rather than the newer bridge. It felt so romantic, that Helen and I had to keep pinching ourselves.

We stopped at a small hotel as close to the house as we could find and finally the morning of Mum's birthday arrived. It was a sunny, windy Saturday. We had hired a car to get around and it was agreed that I would drop Helen off at Dugald's so that she could get dressed there. I had still not seen the dress that Helen had adapted herself for the occasion. I went back to the hotel and got myself dressed too. Finally it was 11.45 a.m. and I made the slow drive back up the coastal road towards the house. Being a few minutes early I pulled the car up beside the spot where I had taken the photograph of the beam of light coming out of the cloud the previous year. I said a few words to Mum before driving on to the house.

I joined the registrar at the front of the house, and stood on the step waiting for Helen to appear. The wind was blowing and at precisely noon Helen appeared from around the side of the house alone, holding a bouquet of flowers. She looked amazing and I was so proud to see the bump in front of her. I knew this was a sad moment for her as she had always wanted to walk down the aisle with her father. She came along the path towards me and we faced one another. It felt as though all the pieces of my life were now being slotted into place and the foundations were being laid for our future. We went through the official part of the ceremony and then we both read out some vows that we had chosen ourselves. We exchanged rings, which felt like a binding agreement; official for all to see. When the registrar finally stated that we were 'now man and wife' I felt my tears fighting to escape. I forced them back and concentrated on the happy feelings, which were now flowing through my body. We kissed and hugged as Dugald's daughter took some photographs. As the registrar took out the wedding certificate for us to sign the wind took hold of it and blew it to the other side of the garden. We laughed about how Mum would find it funny. We then had a special wedding lunch at the little hotel close by, and invited Dugald and his family to join us. This day was going to remain with me for the rest of my life.

The following day we drove over to Inverness to tell Mum's

sisters, who were overjoyed, before heading back down to Leeds on the train to break the news to everyone.

As the due date drew closer it was obvious that the baby was in a standing position and was not going to be coming out by the usual means. The hospital where Helen worked as a midwife arranged for us to have a planned Caesarean a few days before the due date. The staff were extremely kind and managed to find a spare bed for me to put in Helen's room for the few days that she would need to recover from the operation. This meant that I wasn't going to have to go home each night alone, which we both really appreciated.

The midwife, who was a close colleague of Helen's, took her from the room and into theatre, where they gave her something to numb her for the operation. Fifteen tense minutes passed and then the midwife led me down to the theatre where Helen was lying with a green surgical blanket over her. I sat down beside her head and felt the blood draining from my face. This was serious and at the back of my mind I knew that women some-times died in childbirth. I just wanted the baby to be born and for us to be away from all these people and in the safety of our room. I was stroking Helen's head, trying to calm her down, although she was probably calmer than I was.

Then I heard the midwife say, 'Richard, get up, we're nearly there.'

I got up from my chair and walked around so that I could see the doctor putting her hand inside the cut she had made. All of a sudden the baby was being pulled out feet first, completely covered in a white film. There was a slight delay when an arm got stuck but it was quickly released. I could see straight away that we now had a daughter and she was placed on Helen's chest. I rushed back round to the top of the operating table and bent down as I looked into my baby daughter's face. She took a breath and gave out a cry, which sounded beautiful. I felt as though I was looking at a minute version of myself and nothing could have prepared me for the wave of emotion that swept over me in that instant. This was our child; a baby that I never thought I would ever be blessed with and both Helen and I started crying. All three of us were crying and then I thought of Mum and the fact that our daughter would never see her grandmother due to her losing her life at such a young age. I thought about the man who had killed Mum for a brief moment and I felt that such a special moment had been spoilt by what he had done. It was quickly replaced by the thought that Mum was actually living on in our daughter and the joy I had been feeling returned.

As soon as Helen was stitched back up we were taken to our room to be alone with our daughter and Helen breast-fed her for the first time. We decided to call her Skye. We knew it was going to be one hell of a story when we explained to her how she got her name, but it would be a few years before we had to cross that bridge.

A few years ago, Sandra, my counsellor, asked what I would like to be doing in five years' time. This felt pretty much like what I had described. Married to someone I loved, who I trusted and with a family of my own. Now I could see Mum as a person rather than just a memory and a lot of newspaper cuttings. I no longer had to live in the past, because I now knew I had a right to a future and a right to happiness.

Photograph by Alex Durasow, A D Photography

Acknowledgements

I would like to thank the many hundreds of readers of *Just a Boy* who have written to me personally with support and to share their own experiences. Their stories have moved and inspired me, and illustrate how it is possible to overcome the most dreadful of situations.

Thanks to Bev, Alison and Julie Keenen, to Pam and Elizabeth in Uganda, Lorraine, Christine, Jenny and Lara; Mark Metcalfe, Maddi and Simon; Dawn Harrison, Hazel Trudeau, John Meenan for sitting down and explaining that there are many great people within the McCann family, Dugald, Debbie, Caroline, Cameron and Catriona Ross on Skye, Geoff, Helen, Ajay and Khi; Michiel, Mel, Jacob and Daniel Carmel; Kevin, Cathy, Rose and Violet. Thank you Seamus and the rest of 'Nightjar' for the music at our engagement party, as well as Ann and Mike for taking to the stage.

Thank you to the team at SAMM in London, Meg Davies at MBA Literary and, of course, my own literary agent, Judy Chilcote, not forgetting Andrew Crofts for his help once again with my work.

Thank you to Sister Brigid for her help with Mum's memorial service and to Tom from the Leeds Pipe Band for the music on the day. A big thank you to Kev and Delia for providing a much needed stopover on my many journeys to Scotland. I would also like to thank Irving Watkinson and his team at The 1st Detective Agency for their help in our search for other children of Sutcliffe's victims, to Dick Holland for his time, to Jess, Julie and Mark at True North in Leeds for their professionalism in making our film for the BBC, and to David Yallop for his insight into the crimes of Peter Sutcliffe. Thanks to John Bauld for his memories of the morning Mum was discovered; to Suzanne Hallam at Leeds University, Carl Sixsmith for help with my website, to Alex and Janet Durasow for taking what have been some wonderful and memorable photographs over the last two years. I would also like to mention my work colleagues Denise, Cathy, Elaine and Ester who make my shift even more enjoyable. To Jan and Bernice, Maria, Stuart, Michael McNally, Adele, all of the Newlands, Carol Hainstock, Charlie, Chrissie, John Tomey, Micheala and family, Olga, Sandra and family.

Acknowledgements

A special thank you goes to Caroline, Mike, Kerry and Meghan, you are like family to me. A special mention to Sonia for her input into both my books. I love you. Another thank you to Eileen Moxon and her husband Paul, to the Chapmans and Leaders for allowing me into their family. Lastly, a thank you to Hannah and the rest of the team at Ebury for the opportunity of writing this, my second book.

To learn about Richard's next book
and his other products, please log on to:
www.richardmccann.co.uk

SAMM (Support After Murder and Manslaughter)
Registered Charity No: 1000598
Cranmer House, 39 Brixton Road, London SW9 6DZ
www.samm.org.uk

SAMARITANS
Registered Charity No: 219432
Tel: 08457 90 90 90 (24 Hours)
www.samaritans.org